THE **BOYS** WHO **CHALLENGED** **HITLER**

KNUD PEDERSEN AND THE CHURCHILL CLUB

Eigil Astrup-Frederiksen

Uffe Darket

Mogens Fjellerup

Helge Milo

Børge Ollendorff

Jens Pedersen

Knud Pedersen

Mogens Thomsen

THE BOYS WHO CHALLENGED HITLER

KNUD PEDERSEN
AND THE CHURCHILL CLUB

PHILLIP HOOSE

Farrar Straus Giroux
New York

Farrar Straus Giroux Books for Young Readers
175 Fifth Avenue, New York 10010

Text copyright © 2015 by Phillip Hoose
Maps copyright © 2015 by Jeffrey L. Ward
All rights reserved
Printed in the United States of America
Designed by Roberta Pressel
First edition, 2015
5 7 9 10 8 6 4

macteenbooks.com

Library of Congress Cataloging-in-Publication Data
Hoose, Phillip M., 1947–
    The boys who challenged Hitler : Knud Pedersen and the Churchill Club / Phillip Hoose. —
First edition.
        pages cm
    Summary: "The true story of a group of boy resistance fighters in Denmark after the Nazi
invasion"—Provided by publisher.
    Includes bibliographical references and index.
    ISBN 978-0-374-30022-7 (hardback)
    ISBN 978-0-374-30272-6 (ebook)
    1. Pedersen, Knud, 1925–2014—Juvenile literature.   2. Churchill-klubben (Ålborg, Denmark)—
History—Juvenile literature.   3. World War, 1939–1945—Underground movements—
Denmark—Juvenile literature.   4. Boys—Political activity—Denmark—Biography—Juvenile
literature.   5. Middle school students—Political activity—Denmark—Biography—Juvenile
literature.   6. Heroes—Denmark—Biography—Juvenile literature.   7. Sabotage—Denmark—
History—20th century—Juvenile literature.   8. Government, Resistance to—Denmark—
History—20th century—Juvenile literature.   9. Denmark—History—German occupation,
1940–1945—Juvenile literature.   I. Title.
D802.D4H645 2015
940.53'489083—dc23
                                                                                                2014026101

Farrar Straus Giroux Books for Young Readers may be purchased for
business or promotional use. For information on bulk purchases please
contact Macmillan Corporate and Premium Sales Department at
(800) 221-7945 x5442 or by email at specialmarkets@macmillan.com.

For young people everywhere
who find the courage
to make up their own minds

CONTENTS

Maps

THE BOYS WHO
CHALLENGED HITLER

KNUD PEDERSEN AND THE CHURCHILL CLUB

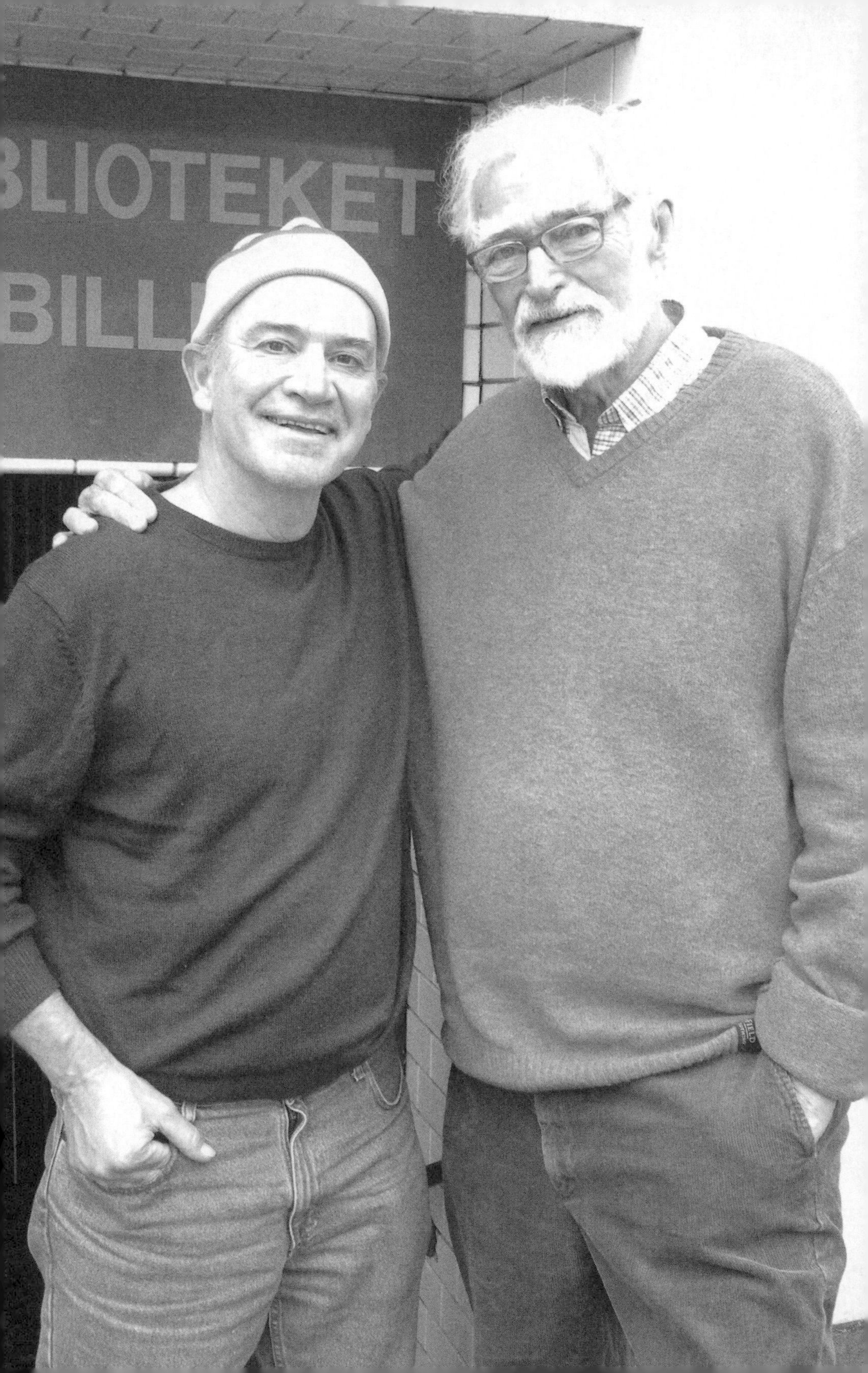
BLIOTEKET
BILL

INTRODUCTION

IN THE SUMMER OF 2000 I TOOK A BICYCLE TOUR OF DENMARK. ON THE FINAL day I visited the Museum of Danish Resistance in Copenhagen, the nation's capital. German forces had occupied Denmark between 1940 and 1945, and the Danes are known for having put up a staunch resistance to their occupiers. One of the most dramatic episodes in all of World War II was the famous Danish boatlift of most of the nation's Jewish population to Sweden in late 1943, just before German forces could round them up and pack them by rail to death camps.

But what isn't so well-known is that resistance in Denmark took quite a while to get off the ground. Exhibits at the museum showed that for the first two years most Danes felt hopelessly overwhelmed by the German Goliaths. They kept hope alive by gathering in public spaces to sing patriotic Danish songs or by purchasing "King's Badges," pieces of jewelry that identified the wearer as a proud Dane.

Then I came upon a special little exhibit entitled "The Churchill Club." With photos, letters, cartoons, and weapons such as grenades and pistols, the exhibit told the story of a few Danish teens, schoolboys from a northern city, who got the resistance started. Mortified that Danish authorities had given up to the Germans without fighting back, these boys had waged a war of their own.

Most were ninth-graders at a school in Aalborg, in the northern part of Denmark called Jutland. Between their first meeting in December 1941 and their arrest in May 1942, the Churchill Club struck more than two dozen times, racing through the streets on bicycles in well-coordinated hits. Acts of vandalism quickly escalated to arson and major destruction of German property. The boys stole and cached German rifles, grenades, pistols, and ammunition—even a machine gun. Using explosives stolen from the school chemistry lab, they scorched a German railroad car filled with airplane wings. They carried out most of their actions in broad daylight, as they all had family curfews.

The author (left) with Knud Pedersen outside the Art Library in Copenhagen, 2012

The Churchill Club's sabotage spree awakened the complacent nation. One photo at the museum showed eight boys standing shoulder to shoulder in a jail yard, all but one holding up a number as a guard looked sternly on. Another snapshot captured the boys posing in front of an ancient monastery, identified as their headquarters. They looked cocky and innocent; one was smoking a pipe. A few were clearly some time away from their first shave. This group of students looked like the last people you'd expect to risk their lives in daring raids against Nazi masters. That charm was surely part of their power. You could imagine them running errands for freight-yard guards to soften them up.

The museum curator said a few of the boys—now old men—were still alive. Knud Pedersen, he said, was the best-known and most knowledgeable of the survivors. He ran an art library downtown. The curator wrote Mr. Pedersen's e-mail address on a business card, which I tucked into my coat.

A week later, back in the United States, I fished out the card and wrote a message to Knud Pedersen. I wondered if the Churchill Club story had been written in English.

Mr. Pedersen's reply came within hours:

> Dear Phillip Hoose,
>
> Thank you for your interest in the story about the Churchill Club . . . but unfortunately a contract has been signed with another American writer . . . I am sorry that I'm not in a position to help you.

So that was that. Someone had beaten me to the story; it wasn't the first time. I printed out our e-mail correspondence, tucked it in a file, and forgot about it for more than a decade.

FAST-FORWARD TO SEPTEMBER 2012. I WAS BETWEEN BOOKS AND LOOKING FOR A new project. Rifling through old papers, I came upon a little manila folder labeled "Churchill Club." Inside I found the long-ago exchange with

Knud Pedersen—among the first e-mail messages I had ever written or received. I wondered if he was still alive and in good health. I also wondered if the other American writer's book had ever been written. It seemed like something I would know about if it had. I jotted a reintroductory message to Knud Pedersen at the ancient address, pushed the Send button, and turned off the laptop for the day.

The following morning a message from Knud Pedersen was waiting: the other writer had not come through, he said. Now he was free to work with me. Immediately. "When can you come to Copenhagen?" Knud wanted to know. I glanced at my calendar and typed, "Oct 7 to 14." Seconds after I'd sent my e-mail, you could almost hear his reply rocketing across the Atlantic: "My wife, Bodil, and I will meet you at the airport. You will stay with us at our cottage."

I booked the flight.

TWO WEEKS LATER MY WIFE, SANDI, AND I WERE MET AT THE COPENHAGEN airport by a white-haired man, half a head taller than anyone else in baggage claim, and his wife. Knud dressed with the dash of an artist. Though we were jet-lagged, he drove us immediately to the Kunstbiblioteket (Art Library), which he had founded in 1957. The library is a below-street-level warren of rooms, some of which contain hundreds of paintings, kept off the ground in wooden racks. For a small lending fee, a patron can take out a painting for a period of weeks, just as one can take out a book at a library. If the borrower falls in love with the painting, he or she can buy it for a reasonable price—the artist has already agreed to sell it. The Art Library stems from Knud's firm belief that art is like bread, an essential ingredient for nourishing the soul. Why should paintings only be available to the rich? And so he started this modest underground library. It was the first art library ever created, now beloved in Copenhagen and world-famous.

While Bodil and Sandi went off to see some local sights, Knud wanted to get right to work. We pulled his office door closed and settled into chairs on opposite sides of a desk. I placed a recording device on the center of the desk and turned it on. We barely budged for the next week—I got very used to Knud Pedersen's face, and he mine. In all we spoke for nearly twenty-five hours, pausing only for meals or to take a walk.

Since I remembered just a few Danish words from my bicycle tour so long before, we had to rely on Knud's English. Knud is a fluent speaker, but conducting a weeklong conversation in his second language clearly fatigued him. Still, he never complained.

That week Knud told me the story of middle-school students who refused to surrender Denmark's freedom no matter what the country's adult leaders did or said. German warplanes buzzed Denmark on April 9, 1940, dropping leaflets informing Danes that their nation had just become a "protectorate" of Germany. The German occupation was presented to Danish authorities as a choice: Comply, give us your food and transport system, work for us, and we'll leave your cities standing. You can continue to police and govern yourselves. We'll even buy materials and goods from you. You'll make money. You'll learn to like us. And after the war you'll share in a glorious future with us. Or you can resist and be demolished. Denmark's king and political leaders accepted.

On the very same day, Germany invaded Norway. Unlike the Danish, the Norwegians fought back early on. When Hitler demanded that Norway surrender, the Norwegians officially replied, "We will not submit voluntarily: the struggle is already in progress." Skirmishes erupted throughout the Norwegian countryside and at sea. Germany captured key Norwegian ports and cities, but the Norwegian army kept fighting, moving inland to take up positions in Norway's rugged interior. Losses were heavy.

As these events transpired, fourteen-year-old Knud Pedersen, a lanky schoolboy growing up in the industrial city of Odense, Denmark, experienced deep emotions, some for the first time. He was at once outraged by the German invasion, inspired by the Norwegians' courage, and ashamed of the Danish adults who had taken Hitler's deal.

Knud and his brother Jens, a year older, gathered a group of boys around them and vowed to fight back—to achieve what they called "Norwegian conditions." When the Pedersen family moved to a different city, Aalborg,

Knud and Jens organized a new group of brave and like-minded classmates to perform acts of sabotage. While most students were oblivious, these few stormed the streets of Aalborg on their bicycles to try to even the score. They called themselves the Churchill Club, after Britain's leader Winston Churchill, whose fighting spirit they admired. The German occupiers, first annoyed and then enraged, called for the speedy arrest and punishment of whoever was stealing their weaponry and destroying their assets. Move fast, they warned Danish authorities, or the Gestapo will take over police functions. The chase was on. The events, which became widely known, awakened and inspired Danes everywhere.

German transport planes flying over Danish rooftops (above) and dropping propaganda on Copenhagen (below), April 9, 1940

1

OPROP!

APRIL 9, 1940. IT WAS A BREAKFAST LIKE ANY OTHER UNTIL THE DISHES STARTED to rattle. Then an all-alert siren pierced the morning calm and the sky above Odense, Denmark, thundered with sound. The Pedersen family pushed back their chairs, raced outside, and looked up. Suspended above them in close formation was a squadron of dark airplanes. They were flying ominously low, no more than three hundred meters above the ground. The black marks on each wing tagged them as German warplanes. Scraps of green paper fluttered down.

Knud Pedersen, fourteen, stepped over and plucked one from the lawn. "OPROP!" it began. Slightly misspelled, that meant something like "Attention!" in Danish. Though the leaflet, addressed to "Danish Soldiers and the Danish People," was written in an error-filled garble of German, Danish, and Norwegian, the point was unmistakable. German military forces had invaded Denmark and were now occupying the country. The leaflet explained that they had arrived to "protect" the Danes from the sinister English and French, that Denmark had become a "protectorate" of Germany. So there was no need to worry: everyone was protected now. Danes should go on with their lives as usual.

OPROP!

Til Danmarks Soldater og Danmarks Folk!

Uten Grund og imot den tyske Regjerings og .det tyske Folks oprigtige Ønske, om at leve i Fred og Venskab med det engelske og det franske Folk, har Englands og Frankrigets Magthavere ifjor i September erklæret Tyskland Krigen.

Deres Hensigt var og blir, efter Mulighet, at treffe Afgjørelser paa Krigsskuepladser som ligger mere afsides og derfor er mindre farlige for Frankriget og England, i det Haab, at det ikke vilde være mulig for Tyskland, at kunde optræde stærkt nok imot dem.

Af denne Grund har England blandt andet stadig krænket Danmarks og Norges Nøitralitet og deres territoriale Farvand.

Det forsøkte stadig at gjøre Skandinavien til Krigsskueplads. Da en yderlig Anledning ikke synes at være givet efter den russisk-finnske Fredsslutning, har man nu officielt erklæret og truet, ikke mere at taale den tyske Handelsflaates Seilads indenfor danske Territorialfarvand ved Nordsjøen og i de norske Farvand. Man erklærte selv at vilde overta Politiopsigten der. Man har tilslut truffet alle Forberedelser for overraskende at ta Besiddelse af alle nødvendige Støtepunkter ved Norges Kyst. Aarhundredes største Krigsdriver, den allerede i den første Verdenskrig til Ulykke for hele Menneskeheden arbeidende Churchill, uttalte det aapent, at han ikke var villig til at la sig holde tilbake af »legale Afgjørelser« eller nøitrale Rettigheder som staar paa Papirlapper«.

Han har forberedt Slaget mot den danske og den norske Kyst. For nogen Dager siden er han blit utnævnt til foransvarlig Chef for hele den britiske Krigsføring.

4a

Propaganda leaflet dropped across Denmark by German planes, April 9, 1940

Knud looked around at his neighbors. Some, still in their pajamas, appeared dazed. Others were furious. Across the street a father and his two sons stood at rigid attention on their apartment balcony, right arms thrust reverently upward toward the German planes. Mr. Anderson, the merchant who sold Tarzan comics from his kiosk on the corner, was shaking his fist at the sky. All four neighbors would be dead within three years.

The following day Denmark's prime minister, Thorvald Stauning, and the Danish king, Christian X, put their signatures to an agreement allowing Germany to occupy Denmark and take control of the government. A terse proclamation explained Denmark's official position:

> The government has acted in the honest conviction that in so doing we have saved the country from an even worse fate. It will be our continued endeavor to protect our country and its people from the disasters of war, and we shall rely on the people's cooperation.

All day long German soldiers poured into Odense and other cities by boat, plane, tank, and transport wagon. Ordinary German foot soldiers of the German defense force—the Wehrmacht—wore brownish-green uniforms with black hobnail boots and rounded green helmets. Well prepared, they quickly took over the town, setting up barracks and command centers in hotels, factories, and schools. They pounded German-language directional signs into public squares and strung miles of telephone lines between headquarters, operations centers, and barracks. By the end of the day, there were sixteen thousand Germans on Danish soil and Germany was in total control.

A German soldier in Copenhagen, April 9, 1940

Operation *Weserübung*

Just after dawn on April 9, 1940, a merchant ship that normally carried coal sailed by Danish security forces and docked at Langelinie Pier, in Copenhagen. Like the Trojan horse of Greek mythology, it carried a secret: hatches opened and German soldiers poured from the hull, fanning out through the city, seizing control of key installations. At the same moment, German forces were invading other Danish cities, pouring in by air, sea, rail, and even (to secure a strategically important airport in the key city of Aalborg) paratrooper. This well-coordinated invasion, which also targeted Norway, had the German code name Operation *Weserübung* (after the Weser river in northern Germany). It was over by noon. Danish forces were stunned and overwhelmed.

When darkness fell, the Wehrmacht took to the streets of Denmark to explore their new home. In Odense, Denmark's third-largest city, many Danish merchants were delighted to open taps of beer or sell pastries to German troops—in fact, the huge new market seemed a windfall. German soldiers pushed into Odense's theaters, taverns, bakeries, and cafés.

In the evenings, the Wehrmacht soldiers marched arm in arm through Odense's streets, weapons strapped to their shoulders, bellowing folk songs in unison as onlooking Danes cocked their heads in curiosity. Knud Pedersen watched from the crowd: "The commander would shout 'Three! Four!' and they would all begin to sing. Some songs were romantic ballads, others military marches. Either way they looked ridiculous. They actually seemed to believe that we liked them. They behaved as if we wanted them there, as if we had been waiting for them, like we were grateful to them."

A TALL, SLENDER TEEN, KNUD PEDERSEN HAD KNOWN AND CARED LITTLE ABOUT war or politics until that Friday morning in April. He was a reasonably good student and handy with his fists, as you had to be at his all-boys school. But Knud's real loves were drawing and painting. Each Saturday morning he met his favorite cousin, Hans Jøergen Andersen, at the Odense library. They went straight for the big volumes of art history, flipped to the breathtaking nudes of Rubens or to Greek sculptures of the female figure, and started drawing. To Knud and Hans Jøergen, the half-draped Venus de Milo was a hundred times more interesting than the fully clothed Mona Lisa.

On Sundays, after Knud's father, the Reverend Edvard Pedersen, completed his Protestant church service, the Pedersen family would convene in the church residency with aunts, uncles, and cousins from other branches, forming a great tribe. In the office, uncles drank and swore their way through a fast-moving, table-slamming card game called l'hombre. Knud's mother, Margrethe, and his many aunts occupied the sitting room, knitting, sipping tea, and talking nonstop, getting up now and then to tend the slow-cooking chickens whose aroma grew stronger from the kitchen by the minute. Children, including Knud, his brother Jens (a year older), his sister, Gertrud (two years younger), and his much younger brothers, Jørgen and Holger, played on the second floor, creating and painting scenery for the evening performance of *Robin Hood* or *Snow White* or *Robinson Crusoe*. Each child got to invite a friend. By evening there were dozens of laughing, drinking, applauding friends and family, full and satisfied. It was like growing up in a cocoon.

Hans Jøergen Andersen

13

Children watching the invaders from a bus

Knud had been only dimly aware that Germany had invaded Poland the year before, and he was oblivious to the special peril that Jews faced with Hitler in control. Before its planes arrived on April 9, Germany had seemed no more than the neighborhood bully, a bordering country with twenty times Denmark's population and an undue influence on Danish history and culture. Even before the war, Danish students had to study German in school, learn German literature, and play German music.

Adolf Hitler had not seemed a particular menace either. In 1937, the fourth year of Hitler's Nazi regime, the Pedersen family had gone on a motor tour of Germany in the family's big green Nash Rambler. As they rolled through neatly cropped pastures and well-managed towns, Knud's parents expressed admiration for what Hitler had accomplished. There was a sense of order and industry in the small towns and cities. Germans were at work while many other nations were still mired in a worldwide economic depression. At the end of the trip their father had pinned a small flag with a swastika to the windshield of the car. When they re-entered Denmark, Danes in the border villages, neighbors who knew the Nazis well, suggested they remove it at once.

But now all this innocence was gone, a bubble popped. German forces had also stormed into Norway on April 9, but Norway had fought back, standing up to the mighty German war machine and paying with a heavy loss of life. In those early days after the German invasion, there were sickening news accounts of Norwegian soldiers slaughtered in defense of their nation. Many were boys in their late teens.

The Invasion of Norway

The German attack on Norway on April, 9, 1940, brought war to Norway for the first time in 126 years. Nearly fifty thousand Norwegian troops were mobilized, but they were overmatched by German forces. Germans quickly seized control of coastal cities and then, deploying troops especially trained for mountain warfare, went after Norwegian soldiers in the country's rugged interior. Norway held out for two months, hoping for support from Great Britain that turned out to be too little and too late.

Norway surrendered after two months of fighting, which had left 1,335 Norwegians killed or wounded. Norwegians kept fighting at sea, employing their large fleet of merchant ships to transport goods to nations at war with Germany. Germany wiped out 106 of 121 Norwegian vessels, killing thousands. Only one of Norway's nine submarines survived the war.

Meanwhile, Danish schoolchildren were being peppered with Nazi propaganda describing the glorious future awaiting them.

KNUD PEDERSEN: I was in eighth grade when the Germans came. We had about two months of school remaining until summer recess. The occupation was on everyone's mind, but during those weeks our teachers kept telling us not to talk about it. Don't object. Don't mouth off. We mustn't arouse the giant. There were many German sympathizers on our school faculty. In Denmark our second language was German, and our books suddenly sprouted all these articles about the happy Hitler Youth who went out in the sunshine and camped and hiked through the forests and played in the mountains and got to visit old castles and all that bloody garbage. It was easy to see that it was all crap.

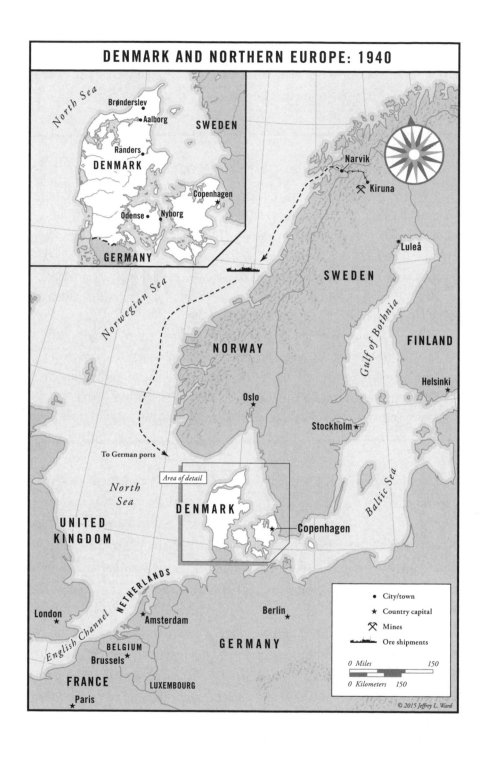

DENMARK AND NORTHERN EUROPE: 1940

North Sea

Brønderslev

Aalborg

SWEDEN

Randers

DENMARK

Copenhagen

Odense

Nyborg

GERMANY

Norwegian Sea

Narvik

Kiruna

Luleå

SWEDEN

FINLAND

Gulf of Bothnia

NORWAY

Oslo

Helsinki

Stockholm

To German ports

Area of detail

North Sea

DENMARK

Copenhagen

Baltic Sea

UNITED KINGDOM

NETHERLANDS

London

Amsterdam

Berlin

English Channel

BELGIUM

Brussels

GERMANY

FRANCE

LUXEMBOURG

Paris

• City/town

★ Country capital

⚒ Mines

⛴ Ore shipments

0 Miles   150

0 Kilometers   150

© 2015 Jeffrey L. Ward

2

The RAF Club

WITH THE OCCUPATION OF DENMARK AND NORWAY, HITLER HAD NOW overwhelmed a second and third nation, the first being Poland in 1939. Denmark may have been tiny, but it was strategically prized by the Nazi regime: the country provided railroad lines to transport iron ore from Sweden and Norway to Germany for use in fashioning weapons. Denmark's fertile farmlands could now feed millions of Germans butter, pork, and beef. Geographically, Denmark stood between Britain and Germany—a valuable buffer. Beyond that, Adolf Hitler regarded Danes as model Aryans. Many were blond and blue-eyed, exemplars of the "master race" Hitler believed in—the perfect people. If Germany could win, Denmark would be a charter member of the world's ruling elite.

KNUD PEDERSEN: A group of us boys in Odense, my older brother, Jens, and my cousins included, started reading the newspapers every day. They were filled with stories of Norwegian civilians being murdered by German troops. The Germans had already started censoring the news, and these reports were supposed to impress readers with the mighty German war machine. But the stories were sickening: twenty-five young Norwegian soldiers rounded up and executed in one town, thirty in another. Wailing families held back by guards. Two young women gunned down in Ringerike. Four unarmed civilians shot at Ringsaker—one of whom was shot in the back, but the bullet went through the neck and came out his jaw. Through all the horror, Norwegians kept fighting.

Jens and I, and our closest friends, were totally ashamed of our government. At least the Norwegian victims had gone down in a country they could be proud of. Our small army had surrendered to German forces within a few hours on April 9. Now there was no armed, uniformed force to stand up for us. We were furious at our leaders. One thing had become very clear: now any resistance in Denmark would have to come from ordinary citizens, not from trained soldiers.

Everything changed in those first weeks, even our family. We had been this settled pastor's family, our lives organized around father's church services. We tried to keep the house quiet as Father puffed on his long pipe in his office and prepared his sermons during the week. Women crowded into our living room to take tea with Mother. Sometimes she could be persuaded to play Mozart on the piano.

Knud Pedersen, a few months before the German occupation. He is front and center, hand to mouth

But after April 9, my father became agitated and defiant. "May God forgive the Nazis," he thundered from his pulpit during his Sunday sermons. "I cannot!" He screened every new friend we brought into the house. "Who is his father?" he would demand. "Is he a Nazi?" My father forbade me and Jens from even asking for a Boy Scout uniform. Hitler Youth wore uniforms. Now Father hated all uniforms.

Edvard Pedersen's Views on Scouting

Boy Scouts and Girl Scouts were very popular in Denmark in the war years. There were at least ten Danish scouting organizations. Sprinkled throughout Denmark's countryside were hundreds of Scout Huts where the groups could gather for camping or rallies. Edvard Pedersen forbade his sons Jens and Knud from becoming Scouts because he distrusted the military aspects of scouting—uniforms, oaths, a command structure. He feared that during the German occupation the Danish Scout movement could be taken over by the Hitler Youth, which delivered a steady stream of German boys—indoctrinated by the hate-filled Nazi ideology of racial and national superiority and trained in a wide variety of military activities such as rifle practice—to the German armed forces.

At night we would gather in his study to listen to radio broadcasts from England. The show from the BBC would begin with the first four notes from Beethoven's Fifth Symphony and then the firm, confident voice that said, "This is London calling." Then war news of aerial battles and troop skirmishes. That was for me.

When school let out for the summer we took our usual family holiday to the western coast of Denmark on the North Sea. It was a total waste for me. I kept asking myself: How on earth could I lie on the beach sunning when my country had been violated? Why were we not as brave as Norway? Had Denmark no pride?

By the time we got back to Odense, in the summer of 1940, Jens and I had reached the same conclusion: if the adults would not act, we would.

· · ·

A FEW DAYS AFTER THEY RETURNED TO ODENSE, KNUD AND JENS MET IN THE quiet calm of the churchyard with their cousin Hans Jøergen Andersen and their friends Harald Holm and Knud Hedelund. The two Knuds were best friends at school, known universally as "Big Knud" and "Little Knud," since Pedersen was nearly two feet taller than Hedelund.

KNUD PEDERSEN: The topic was whether or not to form a resistance unit. My brother Jens thought we should wait a little longer, until we could recruit more members. I felt just the opposite. My idea was to get going—members would come when they saw results. Hans Jøergen was likewise a man of action: he was ready. Harald usually had his head in the clouds about some intellectual problem or another, but this time he was as disgusted with our politicians and the king as we were. "Britain and France will never want us as allies when we make the Germans so comfortable," he kept saying. Little Knud was ready to go—as usual. So our club was voted into existence that day. It was Harald who suggested we call ourselves the RAF Club after the heroic British Royal Air Force.

"So, we exist. Now what do we do?" That's what we all were thinking.

RAF

Throughout the summer and fall of 1940, the boys from Odense listened to radio broadcasts recounting the furious aerial struggle of the Battle of Britain. Their heroes were the pilots of the British Royal Air Force (RAF). Badly outnumbered by the German Luftwaffe, but assisted by air squadrons from Poland, Czechoslovakia, and other nations, the RAF pilots valiantly defended the skies over Britain and kept their country free. The grueling battle claimed many lives. The RAF's success thwarted Hitler's plan to invade the United Kingdom. The pilots' courage prompted British prime minister Winston Churchill to say in the House of Commons on August 20, 1940, "Never in the field of human conflict was so much owed by so many to so few." Deeply inspired, the Odense boys paid them tribute, naming their group the RAF Club.

We were few; the Germans were many. They were fully trained, bulging like goons with their weapons. We had no weapons at all and wouldn't have known how to use them even if we were armed to the teeth. We rode our bikes downtown to the central square to scope things out. Right away we spotted all these freshly planted directional signs. They were yellow and black, not the usual bright red Danish signs. They had black arrows pointing this way and that. Clearly they had just been put up by the Germans to direct the newly arrived soldiers to their barracks and military headquarters. One sign hung suspended from a wooden arm. It was a choice target. Two of us backed up our bikes, counted off, and pedaled full speed at the sign, one on either side, and smashed the thing to the ground. Then we twisted other signs around so they pointed in the opposite directions from what was intended. We were doing these things in broad daylight, right after school. Plenty of people saw us, and we could see them pointing, but we struck lightning-fast and got out of there. In and out quickly—that became RAF Club style.

Our bicycles were our weapons. We carved concentric circles on our bicycle seats to mimic the RAF insignia. We would look with pride at those circles and vow to use our bikes like the British pilots used their

"Our bicycles were our weapons"

planes. Mine was black and rusty, and I called it the Iron Horse. We hung out in front of the Phoenix Cinema in Odense, where they showed westerns. John Wayne had his horse. We had our bikes. Like John Wayne, we were all fast and daring riders.

Hitler and Bicycles

The RAF Club may have been the first saboteurs in Denmark to strike from bicycles, but they were far from the last. The practice increased throughout the war. In October 1944, General Hermann von Haneken, chief of the German high military command in Denmark, ordered all Danish bicycles confiscated. Von Haneken's Nazi political rival Werner Best protested in writing to high Nazi officials, pointing out that since nearly all workers in the food export business rode their bicycles to work, taking bikes away would mean less Danish food for Germans. The delicate issue was finally decided by Adolf Hitler himself. On October 26, Hitler ordered that only unsold bikes from Danish bicycle shops should be confiscated. Hitler sought to keep the action mum, but angry Danes watched German soldiers snatch unlocked bikes from parking lots and fling them into the backs of trucks. Underground papers declared bicycle theft to be "Hitler's secret weapon."

After school the second day we rode back downtown, looking for more ways to disrupt our occupiers. This time we discovered telephone lines linking German military headquarters to the barracks where soldiers slept. They were not electric lines, so there was no danger that we'd fry ourselves if we messed with them. We went out on our bikes, Hans Jøergen, Little Knud, and me, tracing the lines to German-controlled buildings. We found a place next to a tree where the line was only a couple of meters off the ground. It was an easy reach for me. I climbed out on a limb and snipped the wire with garden shears. In the next several weeks we cut those lines again and again.

We struck repeatedly throughout the autumn of 1940, and we began to get a reputation in Odense. We had a particular style. Word got around about the cut wires, and everyone could see the mangled signs. I remember standing in the lobby of the Phoenix Cinema and hearing other kids talking about the saboteurs. Who were they? everyone wondered.

The Germans ordered the Danish police to crack down or else the Germans would take over the police force. That was last thing the Odense police wanted. They assigned eight officers to capture us. Suddenly there were police on the street corners where food was sold at kiosks, asking questions: Did anyone know who cut the lines? Did anyone have any information? The Odense police commissioner ran an announcement in the Odense newspaper offering three hundred Danish kroner to the provider of information leading to our arrest.

Clearly we had their attention: three hundred kroner was three months' wages in a factory back then.

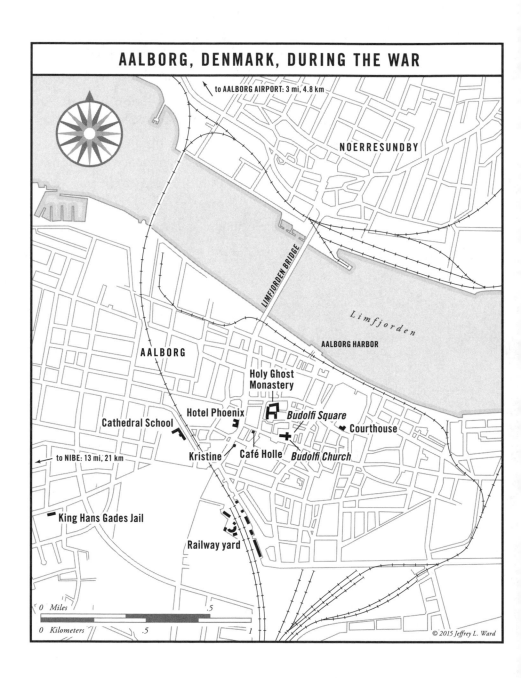

AALBORG, DENMARK, DURING THE WAR

to AALBORG AIRPORT: 3 mi, 4.8 km

NOERRESUNDBY

LIMFJORDEN BRIDGE

Limfjorden

AALBORG HARBOR

AALBORG

Holy Ghost
Monastery

Hotel Phoenix

Cathedral School

Budolfi Square

Courthouse

to NIBE: 13 mi, 21 km

Kristine

Café Holle

Budolfi Church

King Hans Gades Jail

Railway yard

0 Miles   .5

0 Kilometers   .5   1

© 2015 Jeffrey L. Ward

3

The Churchill Club

IN THE SPRING OF 1941, EDVARD PEDERSEN ACCEPTED AN ASSIGNMENT TO A
new Protestant church and moved the family 150 miles north to Aalborg,
a city in the northern part of Denmark called Jutland. Knud and Jens, now
fifteen and sixteen, said reluctant goodbyes to aunts, uncles, and cousins;
to languorous Sunday afternoons of card games and family plays; and,
most important now, to the RAF Club. The Pedersen brothers pledged to
build an even stronger quick-strike sabotage unit in Aalborg. The RAF
boys laughed in their faces. "You'll never keep up with us," they vowed.

Aalborg, Denmark's fourth-largest city, was teeming with German soldiers. The big attraction for the Third Reich's war planners was Aalborg's
strategically located airport. Within minutes on April 9, 1940, the German forces—some parachuting onto the airfield—had secured the airport
and seized all the bridges spanning waterways in Aalborg. They immediately set to work building hangars and expanding runways.

Wagons filled with troops, many soon bound for action in Norway,
raised the dust of Aalborg's streets. German officers took over the best
homes and hotels in Aalborg. Armed Wehrmacht soldiers joined the
Danish population in restaurants, shops, and taverns. Before long, German

soldiers stationed in combat zones enviously called Demark "the Whipped Cream Front." The nickname suggested that German soldiers had it easy in Denmark, especially in contrast to troops on other fronts, where fighting raged.

Why the Aalborg Airport Was So Important

The Aalborg airport, situated in northern Denmark, was essential to the Germans as a refueling station to reach Norway, which they had to control in order to secure ice-free harbors in the North Atlantic. By controlling Norway, the Germans also opened up a route to transport iron ore for making weapons from mines in Sweden, going through the Norwegian port of Narvik. Grand Admiral Erich Raeder, head of the German navy, said it would be "utterly impossible to make war should the navy not be able to secure the supplies of iron-ore from Sweden." The Aalborg airport was therefore one of the most important single assets in all of Denmark. German forces cleverly camouflaged the airfield from attack by British warplanes by carving farm animals out of plywood and scattering the decoys about the grounds. From above, the cows and sheep lying near a green-painted runway suggested a peaceful Danish farm.

Troops awaiting transport at Aalborg

The Pedersen family moved into a drafty, vine-covered medieval structure with a towering loft. Built in 1506, Holy Ghost Monastery, as it was known, was actually a collection of buildings linked by arched passageways. Throughout the centuries the monastery had functioned as a Latin school, a hospital, a church, and the town library. Now it would host Edvard Pedersen's Danish Folkschurch and provide living quarters for the Pedersen family. There was not enough money for electric heating, so each morning Margrethe Pedersen rose before dawn to light the monastery's seven coal furnaces. As she padded down the cold tile hallways carrying her candles, faces of angels, frescoes painted centuries before, peered down from vaulted ceilings above. Hands from the sixteenth century had scratched their initials into the monastery's brick walls.

Holy Ghost Monastery, Aalborg (front)   The "priest yard" of the monastery

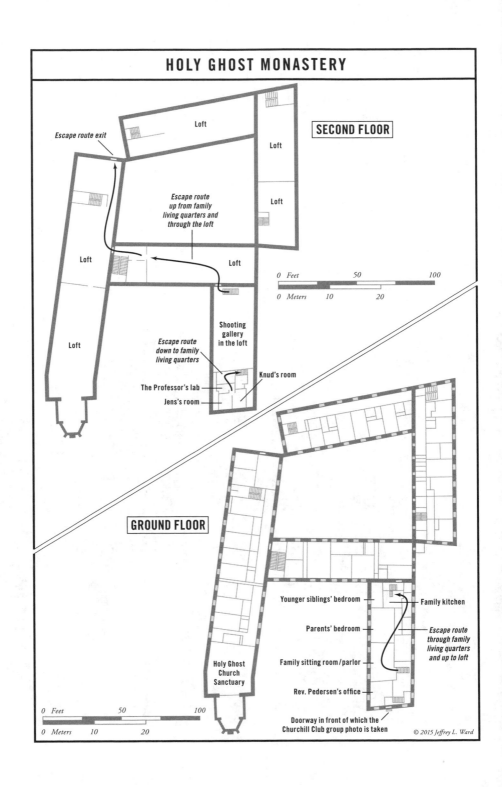

Knud and Jens moved their belongings into adjacent rooms on the second floor. Drawing back his curtain, Knud looked out on a row of freshly polished German roadsters lined up on Budolfi Square outside the Aalborg post office. The vehicles were protected only by a single uniformed guard. If ever there was a perfect target, thought Knud, there it was.

They enrolled at Cathedral School, a college prep school that educated the sons and daughters of the city's leaders. Hundreds of students rode their bikes to school each morning. The young cyclists were sometimes led by an absentminded math teacher who became famous for signaling left turns and then turning right, causing massive pileups.

Though Knud and Jens were eager to resume sabotage activities in Aalborg, they had to move carefully at first. There were pro-German students and faculty members at Cathedral School. It took time to get to know people. Which students could they trust? How to tell?

KNUD PEDERSEN: You couldn't tell who you could count on to join a sabotage unit. No one but Jens and I had any experience. We knew that someone who talks big in a room can panic in the field. My first two friends at Cathedral were Helge Milo and Eigil Astrup-Frederiksen, both in my grade. We had classes together and then started hanging out after school, sometimes at the monastery. Eigil was a sharp character, always well dressed, talking loud and laughing louder, good with the girls. His dad owned a flower shop in the middle of town. Helge came from a well-to-do family in the neighboring city of Noerresundby. His father managed a chemical factory.

After a while I felt I could trust them enough to tell them about the RAF Club and to confide that Jens and I were interested in starting a similar sabotage unit in Aalborg. They wanted in. So one afternoon, as tryout, we three got on our bikes and rode off to cut some phone wires to German barracks. The barracks were in a forest, and naturally there were German soldiers all around.

Both Eigil and Helge panicked once we got close. Please turn around, they begged me. Let's leave the wires for another day. So we did. I could understand—sabotage takes some getting used to. On the way out we pedaled past four German soldiers flirting with a Danish woman, and Eigil and Helge shouted out an insult as they sped by—they called her a "field mattress," a slur for a woman who sleeps around with soldiers. Problem was, my classmates were in front of me and had already passed the Germans, but I hadn't reached them yet. As I whizzed by they took off after us and soon had us surrounded, pinned down, bayonets drawn. They could easily have run us through on the spot. Somehow we talked our way out of it, and they let us go.

Knud's 1941 drawing of a German soldier chasing Cathedral School students in the forest

GERMAN SOLDIERS WERE EVERYWHERE IN AALBORG, IN THE CITY, IN THE FOREST, at the waterfront, thick as flies. Some attended Knud's father's church on Sundays—he struggled with the idea of giving Nazis communion. At

Cathedral School exercise yard, 1943

Cathedral School the gym was converted to barracks for about fifty German soldiers. When the girls from the school exercised in the yard the soldiers hung out the windows whistling and jeering at them.

KNUD PEDERSEN: One day a German officer walked across our schoolyard during our outdoor time. I went over to confront him and informed him he had no business there. We started shouting at each other as boys and soldiers gathered around. Then our rector came flying down the stairs to push me away, shouting, "You idiot! What are you doing? Get back in your classroom!" Nobody blamed him—as head of the school he had to do it or there would have been much worse trouble.

Just before Christmas 1941, a single conversation changed everything. We were in Jens's room at the monastery. It was Jens, me, and four of my fourth-form Middle A classmates: Eigil, Helge, Mogens Thomsen—son of Aalborg's city manager—and Mogens Fjellerup, a pale, pointy-faced classmate who rarely spoke but who was known as the outstanding physics student in our class. Two of Jens's classmates were there, too: a boy named

Sigurd—ranked number one academically in their class—and Preben Ollendorff, a bit of a loudmouth whose dad owned a tobacco factory.

We had just gone out shopping for Christmas presents for our teachers. We were in a great holiday mood, all of us tamping our pipes, laughing about girls, having fun. But as always the conversation snapped back to the German occupation of our country. You couldn't go five minutes back then without returning to the topic on everyone's mind.

The talk turned dead serious. We leaned forward and our voices lowered. We angrily discussed the newspaper articles about the execution of Norwegian citizens and slaughter of Norwegian soldiers who resisted the Nazis. Norwegians were our brothers, we reminded each other, our good neighbors who had the courage to stand up. By contrast, our leaders traded with Germany and sought to placate the Nazis.

Here was the discussion I had longed for! I was thrilled to be with Cathedral students who felt as my brother and I did. These were guys who stayed up like us for the nightly radio broadcasts from England. The more we talked, the angrier we became. It was absurd: if you accidentally bumped into a German on the street, you were expected to strip the hat from your head, lower your eyes, and apologize profusely for disturbing a soldier of the master race. All of us had listened to them braying their idiotic folk songs in the streets.

All this was outrageous, but would anyone do anything about it? Average Danes hated their occupation and occupiers, but ask them to resist and they would say, "No, it cannot be done . . . We will have to wait . . . We are not strong enough yet . . . It would be useless bloodshed!"

The air was thick with our tobacco smoke by the time we laid the proposition on the table. It was the same vow Jens and I and the others in the RAF Club had made back in Odense: *We* will act. *We* will behave as Norwegians. *We* will clean the mud off the Danish flag. Jens and I opened up and told our classmates of our sabotage activities with the RAF Club in Odense. We left with a bounty on our heads, we told them.

The discussion grew heated. The older boys, Sigurd and Preben, wanted nothing of it. "You're crazy," they said. "The Germans will wipe you out in a day! There'll be nothing left of you!" But we younger boys were determined to give ourselves a country we could be proud of.

Together on that snowy afternoon we Middle A classmates, along with Jens, resolved to form a club to fight the Germans as fiercely as the Norwegians were fighting. We would take the resistance to Aalborg. We would call ourselves the Churchill Club, after the great British leader Winston Churchill. Jens volunteered to research the organization of a resistance cell and give us his recommendations, same time, same place tomorrow. Preben and Sigurd vowed not to leak word of our meeting to anyone. Already transformed from the cheerful holiday shoppers we had been an hour before, the Churchill Club stood adjourned.

THE NEXT DAY AFTER SCHOOL, KNUD AND THE OTHER BOYS STOMPED THE SNOW off their boots and tromped into Jens's room in the former priest's wing of the monastery for the first Churchill Club meeting. They draped themselves over a padded sofa and pulled the heavy wooden door shut. Knud took his position on a chair in front of the door to listen for approaching footsteps. And sure enough, they came, followed by a heavy pounding at the door. Knud pulled it open and blinked out at a small blond-headed boy who introduced himself as Børge Ollendorff, Preben's younger brother. Preben had told him about the meeting, and he wanted in. No, he didn't go to their school and, yes, he was younger by a year, but he hated the Nazi swine as much as any of them, and he hated Denmark's official response even more. He stepped past Knud and tossed a bulging tobacco pouch onto Jens's table. Help yourself, he said. He was willing to bring the club a steady supply from his dad's tobacco company. That was powerful. Knud closed the door and sat back down. Børge slid onto the couch.

KNUD PEDERSEN: That afternoon Jens laid out a plan for our club—the model turned out to be very much like professional resistance units later in the war. Even though there were only a few of us to start with, we would divide our work into three departments: propaganda, technical, and sabotage. In time our organization would grow.

The propaganda department would paint up the city of Aalborg with anti-German messages to show that resistance was alive. Since we had no stencil machine or mimeograph to reproduce flyers, our first weapon would be paint. We chose the color blue. Striking quickly from our bicycles we would smear the damning word *vaernemager*—which meant "war profiteer"—on the stores and homes and offices of Danes who were known to be Nazi sympathizers and then pedal away like hell. We would expose them.

We made up our own insignia that day, an imitation of the ridiculous Nazi swastika. Our tilted cross had arrows shooting out of the top of each arm, like thunderbolts. "Here is the symbol of revolution against the Nazis!" our lightning bolts proclaimed. "This flame of rebellion kills Nazis!"

We would apply our trademark blue messages to the polished black German roadsters that lined the streets. We would add cheerful streaks of blue to the drab German barracks and headquarters buildings. Our insignia was also a death warning to the four chief Nazi war criminals, Hitler and his three top henchmen, Hermann Göring, Heinrich Himmler, and Joseph Goebbels.

The technical department would produce bombs and other explosives. We vowed to do serious damage to German assets in the city, especially the railcars filled with airplane parts. We would wipe away Nazi smugness and awaken the Danish people.

In Mogens Fjellerup—nicknamed "the Professor"—we had a unique asset for the technical department. He was so brilliant at physics that the school had given him a key to the physics lab. In the coming weeks and months the Professor would steal heaps of chemical materials to combine into explosives. We nervously took turns helping him mix the ingredients. He spent a lot of time concocting nitroglycerine for bombs. Once he actually spilled the components during a meeting. It was very lucky for us it didn't explode. But we knew we needed weapons, and until we could steal an arsenal we would have to make some of them ourselves. The Professor was the man.

Churchill Clubbers and friends in front of the monastery. Back row (left to right): Eigil, Helge, Jens, Knud. Front row (left to right): unknown, Børge, unknown, Mogens F.

The sabotage department would conduct the on-the-ground field work of the Churchill Club. Of course by being in that room on that day, everyone pledged to commit acts of sabotage—mainly destroying the Germans' assets and stealing their weapons. I naturally gravitated toward sabotage work. I was inclined toward bold action. Jens was more of a planner, though a very brave one. I wanted to make problems, while he wanted to solve them. There was a fair amount of friction between us; we competed at everything.

After heated debate during our first meeting, we also decided to form a fourth section, which we named the passive department. This would consist of schoolmates who were not willing or brave enough to attack in the field but who could help us in other ways, such as raising money or developing support. For example, one classmate was the son of a paint manufacturer. In the coming weeks, once we had really gotten going with propaganda work, this student mentioned in casual conversation that the police had visited his dad's factory seeking a match between the blue paint being slapped all over Aalborg and the company's products. I took a risk and told him about the Churchill Club. I invited him to join. He declined, but he said he'd like to help us. After that he gave us all the blue paint we needed in ten-liter batches. Before long we had ten passive members in all.

We knew that every time we took in someone new, we would risk exposure. But we felt we had to take calculated chances. We needed people.

We concluded our first organizational meeting by agreeing to a few general principles:

- No adults must know of our activities. We would trust only each other.
- No guns in the school—that is, if we ever got any.
- Anyone who mentioned the name of the club to an outsider would be immediately banned.
- And, finally, the most important rule: To be an active member of the Churchill Club one had to commit a serious act of sabotage such as stealing a German weapon.

The reason for the last rule was simple. One who got caught stealing a German weapon stood a good chance of being executed. Risking this, everyone would have a serious investment in the club's work. This rule would discourage anyone from telling authorities about the club because that person, too, would be incriminated. From a legal point of view, we would all be guilty together.

We would continue to meet after school in Jens's studio. We would begin by taking roll and then go out on patrol. We'd divide the city up into sections, patrol on bicycles, and meet back at the monastery to discuss opportunities—then strike if we had anything. We would become daylight-crime specialists, since most of us had family curfews and couldn't be out past dark. No problem—everything was guarded more closely at night anyway. The enemy was vulnerable to daytime strikes. And if we needed to work at night, we would tell our parents that we had formed a bridge club. We could say we were going out in the evening to play cards at the home of the only one of us who didn't have a telephone.

As darkness gathered outside the monastery walls and the hour grew late, I got up, pulled the chair from the door, and said goodbye to my new mates. Today we were born. Tomorrow we would act.

The Churchill Club's insignia, painted everywhere. "This flame of rebellion kills Nazis," it proclaimed

4

Learning to Breathe

IN JANUARY 1942, DENMARK WAS IN ITS SECOND YEAR OF GERMAN OCCUPATION. Danish citizens expressed their opposition to Germany not by fighting back, but by making gestures of national pride. Some gathered in public spaces to sing Danish folk songs. Some purchased "King's Badges," offered in jewelry shops in silver or gold, as a symbol of solidarity with the government. Some students refused to speak German in language classes.

Meanwhile, German soldiers settled in. Month by month the occupiers grew ever more comfortable in Denmark, trading freely with merchants and learning to savor the country's food and culture. Some Danish manufacturers collaborated with their "protectors" by making weapons and parts to facilitate German war plans. Others created temporary housing for the soldiers. One manufacturer, the Riffel Syndicate in Copenhagen, took an order to make five thousand machine guns for the Germans, who paid for it with funds drawn from the Danish National Bank. There was money to be made all around.

In this atmosphere, the Churchill Club began its activities.

A King's Badge

KNUD PEDERSEN: We started our Churchill Club work with a series of daylight raids on German directional signs in Aalborg, as we had in Odense. Often we worked in pairs. With a shrill whistle one would distract a soldier into leaving his post while the other slipped behind and twisted the sign around so that German troops and wagons would circulate to the wrong places. Sometimes we smashed signs to the ground with hammers. The Germans would put them back up, and we would take them back down again. These exercises weren't winning the war, but we were getting practice and our actions were noticed by the people in the streets. Someone was not giving in.

The sign raids also gave us experience working with the threat of arrest hanging over our heads, or the prospect of being shot. You had to get used to it. You had to learn to breathe around armed soldiers. Your body works differently in an atmosphere of danger or excitement. Even the smallest of missions can send your diaphragm into spasms when you have no experience. You start to breathe too fast. Some people laugh uncontrollably. The tongue loosens. Some say things they regret. Ours was a war without fronts, meaning the enemy was 360 degrees around us at all times. Even with our parents, teachers, and classmates, we had to be careful what we said and whom we said it to.

BY FEBRUARY, THE WALLS OF AALBORG WERE STICKY WITH BLUE CHURCHILL Club paint and the German directional signs looked like pretzels. Knud and the other young saboteurs were ready for a bigger target. One candidate was obvious: there was no better-known German collaborator in Aalborg than the Fuchs Construction Company. It built hangars, runways, and office buildings at the Aalborg airport for the German military, receiving handsome profits as it helped the Third Reich make more and more flights to battered Norway. The Fuchs Company was a prime example of everything the Churchill Club hated about the Danish government's compliant posture.

At the Aalborg airport, the company's headquarters was isolated from the terminal and runways. The boys decided to set it ablaze.

KNUD PEDERSEN: Eigil, Helge, Børge, and I went out to perform the raid on a bitterly cold winter evening. It was Eigil's initiation night. If he did well and the operation succeeded, he would become a full-fledged Churchill Club member.

We told our parents we would be playing bridge to gain a few hours more to strike under the cover of darkness. We met outside the monastery and took off two by two toward the most dangerous place in town. The Limfjorden Bridge connects Aalborg with the neighboring town of Noerresundby, spanning a fjord. Because the airport, on the Noerresundby side, was so important to the Germans, they posted armed guards at checkpoints on both sides to examine vehicles. We were waved through both checkpoints without incident and continued north along snow-lined streets out into the countryside.

A few miles later the hulking shapes of the Aalborg airport hangars came into view. The snow-covered airfield, behind a wire fence, looked like a farm, dotted with livestock. But the animals never moved. They were the Germans' wooden decoys, made to create the impression from the air that the traveler was passing over pasturelands rather than airfields of military importance. There was a manned guard post at the main entrance to the airport, but the Fuchs office was off to the side in a darkened region of the facility. The wire fence with the NO UNAUTHORIZED PERSONNEL sign was easy to cut through.

We crept up to the Fuchs headquarters and stood still. There were no lights on inside, and—thankfully—no guard dogs. We stood motionless in the dark for several minutes, listening for a sound of any kind and hesitating, struggling to summon up the courage to do the job and privately reminding ourselves that we could still turn back. Then suddenly Børge grabbed a stick and smashed out three windows. It made a huge noise! When I looked at Eigil I saw a wet stripe running down his trousers.

We went through the windows and found ourselves inside an office filled with desks and drawing tables, lined up in rows. Architectural drawings were stacked on one of the tables. Bills and receipts were held in place by a paperweight on a second desk. Another supported a pile of business cards that read: "You have been visited by a member of the Nazi party."

Overlooking all the desks and chairs was a large framed photo of Adolf Hitler. He glared down coldly at us, as if he knew who we were. We began our own work by liberating the führer from his nail on the wall and smashing him over a desk. Glass flew everywhere. We slammed the portrait onto the floor and took turns dancing on his face. We then gathered all the drawings and receipts and business cards into a single pile, placed what was left of Hitler on top like a cherry on a cake, and placed a pillow atop the whole stack. Just before we lit it we carried out a typewriter—a very useful machine that was difficult to find and almost impossible to buy. We also carried away what turned out to be a leveling machine. We didn't know what to do with it, but it looked promising. Then we put a match to the whole traitorous mess and made a run for our bikes. On our way back we looked behind us and saw a glow forming bright against the darkness through a window. It was a beautiful sight!

At the next day's Churchill Club meeting the others asked if we had left a calling card taking credit for the attack. No, we said, why would we do that? Well, what would keep the Fuchs stooges from assuming they had been raided by common criminals, not patriots? Hard as it was to swallow, our colleagues were right. We had not made it clear that collaboration central had been visited by Danish patriots who would never give in. So we took a sledgehammer and wrecked the leveling machine we had stolen—we couldn't figure out what it did anyway—and wrote a message on it: "Get out of our country, you stinking Nazis." A few nights later we bicycled back out to return the wrecked machine to them, with our auto-graph. We discovered that the Fuchs office hadn't burned down—the building was standing. But it was still satisfying to know that we had de-stroyed their plans, blueprints, and records, which meant that they would have to start over.

And we had greatly improved Hitler's looks.

Crime scene photograph of the damage at the Fuchs Construction Company showing ashes of destroyed design drawings for new airport hangars

King Christian X riding through the streets of Copenhagen during the occupation

5

Flames of Resistance

DENMARK SEEMED A PLACE RIGHT OUT OF A HANS CHRISTIAN ANDERSEN FAIRY tale in the first months of 1942, especially compared to so many other places in the world where bloody conflict was raging. Every morning in Copenhagen, Danish king Christian X took a horseback ride through the streets, saluted by both the Danish citizens and the German soldiers he passed. The Danish minister of foreign affairs, Nils Svenningsen, took his morning rides with the German high commander, Werner Best.

While citizens and soldiers were being shot in Norway, Danish business leaders lunched with German officers, negotiating deals over pastry. Unemployed Danish workers were sent to Germany and given the opportunity to work for the Nazis, while uniformed German soldiers strolled through Denmark's city streets arm in arm with Danish women. In the early months of 1942, it was clear that many Danish officials were expecting a Nazi victory in which Denmark would be a business partner.

Winston Churchill referred to Denmark on the radio as "Hitler's tame canary."

KNUD PEDERSEN: After the Fuchs strike we turned our attention to German vehicles. To our arsenal of blue paint, hammers, and bicycles we added gasoline and matches. Arson became our game. We took to carrying a small quantity of petrol with us when we went out, stuffing the canister in a school bag. As always we specialized in quick strikes—in and out.

One day during our bicycle reconnaissance we found three large German transport trucks unguarded in a field. We crept up to each and raised our eyes above the windows to make sure no one was hiding or sleeping inside. All were empty. Quickly one of us slashed the seats, pulled the stuffing out, and doused it with gasoline. Another painted our iconic blue swastika with lightning bolts on each truck. On a signal, a third tossed a lit match into each cabin and we tore out of there as fast as we could. Flames were instant; petrol made all the difference.

Werner Best (right), the German high commander in Denmark, with Erik Scavenius, the Danish prime minister, 1943

Another afternoon we came upon an unguarded German tractor near the airfield in Lindholm, a suburb of Aalborg. Again we slashed the seats, painted the symbol, and prepared the stuffing but suddenly realized no one had remembered the petrol. We ordered Børge, the youngest of us, to ride back to the monastery and retrieve it. He objected that we should draw straws. We

Danish police photo of German truck vandalized by the Churchill Club

told him to get going. He ignored us and instead opened up the gas tank and threw a lit match into it, igniting the vehicle.

That was classic Børge. He looked the innocent type, the kind of innocent who is the most dangerous. With blond curls, twinkling blue eyes, and a sweet smile, he seemed angelic. But he loved action. He was fearless and smart and very quick on his feet. He was hot-tempered and mouthy as well, which sometimes got us in trouble. He was the youngest of us all—still only fourteen—but I liked him. We shared an irreverent sense of humor. He was a lot like Little Knud had been back in Odense. Both were fearless and both were small.

Børge and I grew close. He lived about fifteen miles to the west of us in a small town named Nibe but went to school in Aalborg. Jens knew his older brother, and that's how he found us. He was so hungry to join us that he often rode his bicycle fifteen miles through snowy streets back and forth between Nibe and Aalborg to be with us.

When an operation called for two, Børge and I often worked together.

We developed a feel for each other, often one that didn't call for words. One would distract, the other would strike. For example, one time Eigil, Jens, Børge, and I came upon several German roadsters lined up behind a fence downtown. We could plainly see a pistol resting on the front seat of the nearest car. It set us drooling. We had to have it.

The Germans had posted a single armed soldier by the fence. Clearly bored, he was absentmindedly watching a few kids play football in the adjacent street. Børge stood still and observed the game intently. When the ball rolled loose in our direction he sprinted after it and kicked it over the fence. The ball came to rest beneath one of the German vehicles. I ran up and asked the guard to please be allowed to fetch it. The soldier stood aside and let me open the gate. Inside, I picked up the ball, and, as Børge occupied the guard with a question, I ran to the car and snatched the gun, stuffing it into my waistband. Then I trotted back out into the street and kicked the ball back to the boys and walked away.

We got better and better at disabling the German vehicles we found throughout Aalborg, especially near the airport. We learned how to pry off a radiator screen in a flash, and either steal or smash the exposed parts. Always we left our signature in bright blue paint.

The vehicles we wanted to destroy most were lined up right outside my room at Budolfi Square. We could see them through the curtain at every Churchill Club meeting. They were an eyesore, an affront, an insult. While winter swirled around the monastery's ancient walls, we gathered in Jens's room debating various schemes for taking them out, even if it meant killing the guard. More and more, weapons became our obsession. It was all we could talk about. Now that we had a pistol and a collection of iron rods we had discovered in the monastery attic, were we really going to use them?

One afternoon through a fog of pipe smoke, we considered a plan for a new strike. The goal would be to decommission the cars outside my window, to make them useless. Two of us would work on the cars, removing radiator screens, pulling and smashing engine parts, while others distracted

German vehicles around Budolfi Square, as seen from Knud's bedroom window

the guard with conversation—"Uh, officer, sir, do you have a light? You don't understand Danish? I'm so sorry, sir. Oh, what is the word for 'matches' in German?"

If the guard detected the operation, a fourth club member, concealed beneath one of the cars, would slip up behind him and smash him in the head with an iron rod. Or, someone suggested, maybe a blow to the neck would be better. Whatever, we would kill him. Once he was dead, we'd drag him under one of the cars. It was agreed. We drew straws to see who would smash the guard. The winner—or loser—sat down and turned the rod over and over in his hands trying to picture himself using it.

But we didn't do it. Two members who were not present during the planning session objected when they heard about it. "Hit a man from behind? That's not us! That violates our code. It is cowardly, even if the target's a German!"

Back when we had started the club, we all vowed that we could, and would, kill. But when the time came we were woefully unprepared. We were middle-class kids—sons of professionals, boys who had never shot a gun or wielded a club or slit a throat. We had no military training—we were too young to enlist in the army, and our army barely existed now anyway. We had no experience with the feelings involved in taking a life. A typical military inductee went through basic training or boot camp, where one's personality was stripped to the core, desensitized to accept the horror of war as part of the job, and rebuilt as a warrior. For us—young patriots having to invent and train ourselves as we went along—it would take more time and preparation to be ready to kill.

So the Budolfi car mission was postponed but not scrapped. We would just have to work up to it. Our aborted mission was bitterly disappointing, though, especially when Jens received a coded letter from our cousin Hans Jøergen in Odense. To be safe, Jens and Hans Jøergen had developed a code for trading war bulletins. Marie Antoinette had used the same code pattern, which Jens and Hans Jøergen had modernized so it could be deciphered with the words "Denmark expects every man to do his duty."

Hans Jøergen wrote that the RAF Club had just destroyed fifteen German cars in Odense—exactly what we had failed to do at Budolfi Square. Details were sketchy, but it was clear Hans Jøergen had been the leader. The target was a converted riding stable filled with German automobiles and other war materials. They struck on the evening of an all-day Boy Scout assembly. Hans Jøergen—a Boy Scout—had spent the day dressed in his full scouting uniform, eagerly taking part in troop activities so everyone would see him and remember that they saw him there.

Just after dark Hans Jøergen slipped out of the assembly hall and rode his bike to the stable. The guard usually posted outside the door had been removed by an RAF Club sympathizer, a girl who had flirted him away from his post. Hans Jøergen tiptoed inside and, using some sort of homemade bomb, ignited a quantity of straw. He then anonymously telephoned the fire department to report a fire on the opposite side of Odense. Then, still in his uniform, he beat it back to the scouting forum to rejoin his mates. The fire brigade swallowed the bait and clanged off to the wrong end of town. All those lovely roadsters, reported Hans Jøergen in his message to Jens, had over an hour to burn into charred steel sculptures.

It was a bold stroke. Hans Jøergen proudly claimed that the RAF Club had pulled ahead of the Churchill Club. We had no argument to offer. All we could do was try to match it.

German vehicles destroyed by RAF Club action, Odense

An interior passageway in Holy Ghost Monastery, a sprawling old building perfect for secret meetings

6

To Arms

As winter snows began to melt in the spring of 1942, the Churchill Club expanded into a force with nearly twenty members, active and passive. Though they continued to seek out targets after school, they made more nighttime raids, mainly attacks on German vehicles, conducted while they were supposedly playing bridge. One of the club's most important new active members was Uffe Darket, whom Eigil had known from another school. When Eigil had transferred to Cathedral School he stayed in touch with Uffe and recommended him to the Churchill group. At first glance, no one would have taken Uffe for a saboteur, for he was always neatly dressed, respectful, and pleasant. His blond good looks and steady manner inspired calm and trust. But like the others, he was brave and dedicated—and angry. He was quickly accepted.

Knud and Jens Pedersen took great pains to keep the Churchill Club secret from the rest of their family. The brothers knew that if their parents had any idea what was going on they would move to stop it. In some ways, it wasn't that hard a secret to keep: their parents, Edvard and Margrethe, were absorbed in the countless details of church work. Their younger sister, Gertrud, was no more interested in Jens's and Knud's lives than they were in hers. Little brothers Jørgen and Holger were still in elementary school.

It helped that Jens's and Knud's rooms—headquarters of the Churchill Club—were at the top of a staircase, isolated from the rest of the family's living quarters. During their meetings, the boys were careful to post a guard at Jens's door to make sure no one came up the stairs. All in all, the Pedersen parents were delighted their sons had made new friends so quickly after their move to Aalborg.

Likewise, most Cathedral School students had no idea what was going on. "Knud Pedersen would fight," a classmate later wrote. "Soon he gathered from class a bunch of boys around him. They went mostly around the schoolyard as a closed flock without the rest of us knowing why." Cathedral School faculty members continued to drill their students in preparation for midterm exams, unaware of the greater drama in which a few of their students were involved.

Even as the club got more and more proficient at stealing weapons, they continued to try to manufacture their own explosives. The Churchill Club's "Professor"—Mogens Fjellerup—converted an elevated chamber on the monastery's second floor into a chemical laboratory. There, he mixed combustible materials smuggled from Cathedral School's chemistry classroom. In the beginning, they fizzled out again and again. But with each failure, the Professor felt he was getting closer.

KNUD PEDERSEN: Sometimes the whole second floor was thick with smoke and we had to run gagging to throw open the upstairs windows. The Professor was trying to make small handmade bombs to drop into the motors of parked German cars. For a while they just went *ppsssst* and we had to pry off the radiator screens and smash the engines with ordinary tools. But the Professor kept at it. He was the silent type who only gave a faint smile when the rest of us were doubling over with laughter.

We made up our operations as we went along, sometimes taking chances that we shouldn't have taken, but we had no formal command structure. We were too jealous of each other to name or elect a leader. We belittled each other. The Professor reddened when Eigil insisted his bombs didn't qualify him for full Churchill Club membership—he had to steal a gun like everyone else. Others piled on.

"Yeah, your 'bombs' never work anyway."

"What a mastermind!"

The sarcasm was as thick as the monastery walls, but we had faith in each other and our mission held us together. We were out to install "Norwegian conditions"—the courage to resist—in our country. Denmark would stand whether the government liked it or not.

Several times a week we met in Jens's room, took roll, and then went out on our bikes. We divided the city into quadrants and scouted, sometimes in pairs and sometimes alone. We inspected the parked German vehicles and buzzed by the Wehrmacht offices, searching for German assets to destroy and weapons to steal. Sometimes we came up empty. Usually there was something.

During one of these routine reconnaissance missions, I drifted past a German barracks and saw something that made my eyes nearly pop out of my head. It was almost too good to be true! I stood up from my bicycle seat and mashed down the pedals, tearing around town, rounding up the others and telling them to get back to the monastery at once. Within minutes we were on Jens's couch, with Børge's tobacco glowing in our bowls, a chair wedged against the door and all eyes on me.

"So what's the big deal?" came the question.

"Big deal is, I found a lovely German rifle dangling from a bedpost inside a barracks bedroom. The window is wide open. It's ours for the taking. Now's our chance."

There was unanimous agreement—we had to have it. "Let's wait for night," someone said. But the rest of us knew we had to move now, in broad daylight. The streets would be crowded, providing cover. The building was unguarded, or at least it had been an hour ago. At night there would be a German on that bed. Now there was only a rifle.

No, we would make a daylight strike. But if we were able to snatch the rifle, we would have to conceal it as we transported it back to the monastery. A Danish boy couldn't just be seen cheerfully pedaling down a Wehrmacht-filled Aalborg street with a German rifle slung over his shoulder. So we had to make one plan for capturing it and another for moving it.

Our operation called for three boys and a raincoat. It was about three o'clock when Børge, Mogens Thomsen, and I reached the barracks. We circled the block a couple of times, just to see how traffic was moving and to make sure there were no German guards posted. It was still clear. On the third lap Mogens let himself fall behind a little, while Børge and I advanced, with Børge carrying the coat. Close to the barracks, we ditched the bikes behind a tree. The barracks building was enclosed by a barbed-wire fence, but the strands were widely separated and easy to step through. I held the fence open for Børge, then let myself in and walked slowly toward the window. The rifle was still there, dangling on a belt from the post of an empty bed. But in the next room, his back to us, was a German soldier, busily polishing his windows with a rag! He hadn't seen us—yet.

We froze in place and waited for our hearts to calm down. Then we exchanged nods, and I made my move. I slipped to the corner of the building, inched to the window, and reached inside for the rifle. I wrapped my hand around it, snatched it off the bedpost, and passed it out to Børge. The weapon was almost as long as he, but Børge got it bundled inside the coat and began walking away—not running, just an even stride. As I backed away I could hear the German next door, still rattling the room with the fury of his window washing. In a flash we were back over the fence and Mogens had the rifle wrapped in the raincoat on his bike. A postman and two women stood on the street staring at us as we took off. I met one of the women's eyes. They told me she had seen the whole thing. She appeared conflicted. Would they start yelling or hold their tongues? We didn't hang around to plead our case, but we didn't hear any kind of alarm behind us as we rode away.

We took narrow streets back to the monastery. Again and again Mogens had to stop to readjust the coat, because both ends of the rifle kept sticking out. When the monastery came in sight, we whistled our arrival, threw the bikes against the gate, and ran the bundle inside. We lowered the coat onto Jens's bed and unwrapped the prize. It was a beautiful rifle, the stock polished and the barrel clean. Now we had a significant weapon, a long-range killing machine. We had to sort out what it meant but not right now. The three of us were exhausted. We called a meeting for the following afternoon. It would be the most important yet.

THE CHURCHILL CLUB HAD FULL ATTENDANCE THE NEXT DAY. THE MEETING began with a detailed report of the rifle's liberation, from the window-washing Nazi to the witnesses. Everyone got to hold the weapon, look down its barrel, feel the balanced weight of the deadly machine, and imagine a Nazi within its sights. All of the boys shared in the satisfaction that at least one good weapon had changed sides of the ledger.

Then the discussion became more serious.

Barracks of a Danish volunteer army corps that assisted the German army
with guard duty and sabotage prevention

KNUD PEDERSEN: We had done something different yesterday, more significant than anything we'd done yet. Yes, the pistol we'd stolen from the German car downtown was important, but a pistol offers only a few shots at close range. A rifle would let us snipe, to attack or cover each other from long distance.

We had reached a crossroads. The question before us was: Should we continue along the same path, defacing and destroying German property, or should the main job of a Churchill Clubber now be to build a cache of weapons and train ourselves to use them against our German occupiers? To choose the latter would not mean that we would cease to burn their cars and buildings. But our new emphasis would be weapons.

It was a spirited discussion, with everyone joining in except the Professor, who rarely said anything. But in the end we agreed that if our goal was to awaken Denmark, we must get weapons. And as our operations increased in scale and complexity, we would need firepower to cover each other. Finally, if the war turned in our favor and British troops came to liberate us from Germany's grasp, wouldn't it be great to have weapons to share with British troops on the day their fighting forces arrived to liberate us? With weapons, we would be able to fight side by side with our allies. In the end we were of one heart: in the words of the French national anthem, *"Aux armes, citoyens!"* "To arms, citizens!" Weapons! We must get weapons!

But where to find them? One kid proposed that if we just kept riding around, other weapons would appear. Look what has just happened for Knud, he said. Another countered with a story about a small boy who had found a dead bird. He buried the bird and, proud of himself, made a cemetery for more dead birds. Then he went out to find others. But he couldn't. Finding the first bird had been a one-time event, a stroke of happenstance and luck. The point of the story was that if we were to develop an arsenal of weapons we couldn't just rely on luck. We had to think strategically about where German weapons were concentrated, and how to get them.

We made a list of the most likely German gathering places where weapons might be lifted. There were always German officers in the pastry shops downtown. The train stations were good for ammunition boxes. The waterfront teemed with armed soldiers. And now that the weather was warming and windows were likely to be open, a regular inspection of German barracks would be a must.

We composed the next day's patrols and adjourned our meeting to go home and study for our midterm examinations.

Parading German soldiers

7

Whipped Cream and Steel

BY THE SPRING OF 1942, AALBORG, WITH ITS AIRPORT AND HARBOR, HAD become a way station for many thousands of German soldiers headed to Norway to safeguard shipments of iron ore from Swedish mines to German factories. Hitler also used Aalborg as a place for German soldiers to rest and recover from battling the Soviet Union on the savage eastern front, where fighting had begun the previous summer.

The eastern front of World War II saw conflict on a colossal scale beginning in June 1941, when Hitler's army invaded Russia. The campaign pitted European Axis powers—led by Germany—and Finland against the Soviet Union, Poland, Norway, and other Allied forces.

It was the largest-scale military confrontation in history. There were ferocious battles, marked by wholesale destruction and immense loss of life due to combat, starvation, exposure, disease, and massacres. Of the estimated seventy million deaths attributed to World War II, over thirty million, including civilians, occurred on the eastern front.

Any German soldier pulled from the eastern front to rest and recover in Aalborg had to count his blessings.

Day by day, German soldiers streamed in and out of the city. Many were bound for Norway, sleeping for a few nights in makeshift barracks set up in schools and churches until they were ordered onto transport ships. Each soldier was armed, and each weapon was now an object of interest to the Churchill Club. The boys in the club soon found they were just as good at stealing weapons as they were at arson. "Getting guns was no trick at all," one of the boys later recalled. "We'd accost soldiers after a parade or at a railway station and while a couple of us engaged them in friendly conversation, the others would steal the rifles they'd propped against a wall or bench."

KNUD PEDERSEN: Day by day our arsenal of stolen knives, guns, and bayonets grew. We hid them in the monastery basement and went down to check on them all the time. Our parents never caught on. Mother and Father were alarmed by my sliding grades, but they were happy to see me make new friends and probably took it as a good sign that we all spent so much time at the monastery rather than at someone else's house.

Germans kept arriving in Aalborg. The rows of their vehicles that lined the streets grew longer and longer. They seized the best hotel in town— the Hotel Phoenix—as their command center.

At the docks we observed hundreds of German soldiers marching down to Aalborg harbor and lowering themselves into the bottoms of old freight ships bound for Norway. As much as we hated the Germans, it was hard not to have a little feeling for the common soldiers heading off to battle. Many of them didn't seem much older than us.

When a ship was fully loaded a net was stretched over the top of the hull so that bodies wouldn't come to the surface if the vessel was sunk by torpedoes from British submarines lying in wait just beyond the Limfjorden. In fact, it became unpopular to eat hornfish, which were green, because it was said they got their color from drowned German soldiers in green uniforms.

We spent a lot of time at the docks, straddling our bikes, arms folded on the handlebars, squinting out like hawks for weapons left unguarded by German soldiers boarding their ships. Sometimes soldiers would lay their weapons on the ground within our reach, and we would snatch them like gulls after crumbs. Their naval officers were always waving their arms and shouting at us to scram, but they never shot at us. We would flee full-speed, and come back in due time.

The focus on weapons simplified our work: we knew what we were after. We became bolder. One day a few of us saw a German officer's car roll to a stop in the middle of a downtown street. The exasperated driver jumped out of the cabin and stormed around front to crank the engine back into life. As he was cranking, Børge ran to the open car door, grabbed his bayonet dangling from a peg inside, and walked away.

It wasn't just small weapons we were after; we had big eyes, too. One evening several of us cycled over the Limfjorden Bridge to Noerresundby with the goal of destroying an antiaircraft cannon—the Germans called it a "flak cannon." It was boldly positioned on the harbor embankment, its great long barrel always thrust toward the sky for all to see. But for all its self-importance, it wasn't guarded at night. Our plan was to hoist it out of its boxlike foundation, carry it down to the docks, and heave it into the Limfjorden.

German planes over the Limfjorden

We had gotten it up out of its box and had just become comfortable with the weight of it when we heard our guard whistle. We dropped the monster and scattered. The threat turned out to be an ordinary Danish cyclist. Chewing out our guard for alerting us for so little, we returned to the box and lifted the cannon again. Staggering, we got it about halfway down to the dock before we heard another whistle. This time it was a German guard, and we could see the barrel of his rifle sticking out of his pack as he carefully made his rounds. That was it. We dropped the cannon and pranced away toward our bikes, swearing loudly at the Germans and using crowbars and hammers to smash the windows of their buildings as we left. He heard us, of course, and gave chase. He turned out to be in great shape! We ran for our lives, ditching our bikes, with the guard bellowing at us to halt and firing shots in the air. That night we stayed in Noerresundby rather than risk the bridge, and the next morning we sneaked back to retrieve our bikes.

LATE IN MARCH THE BOYS STOLE SEVERAL HUNDRED CARTRIDGES FOR THEIR new rifle from a cargo delivery truck at the train depot, by far the best place to find ammunition. They continued to take pistols and bayonets from loosely attended touring cars and open-windowed barracks.

KNUD PEDERSEN: Restaurants were the ripest pickings of all. The Germans had free run of downtown Aalborg, and they really took it over. Booted, helmeted, and heavily armed, they shopped for meat, vegetables, wine, and tobacco alongside ordinary Danes. It was hard to be at ease around them in a small shop, or to defend your position in line against armed goons. Merchants who sold to them were reviled by many as traitors. These storekeepers didn't care; there was money to be made.

Our occupiers were crazy about the local taverns and restaurants. Danes are famous for their pastries, and German officers soon discovered the *konditori* (pastry shop) Kristine, regarded as the finest in Aalborg. Kristine was famous throughout the city for light, delicious whipped cream cakes. Men of the Third Reich removed their hats, hung up their coats and weapons in the cloakroom, and settled into red padded sofas until

Kristine, a *konditori* (pastry shop) in Aalborg where German officers often gathered

they were called to their tables. The officers then slid into high-backed, upholstered wooden chairs, placed their orders, and smoothed fresh linen napkins over their laps. This surely beat the eastern front.

One night four of us slipped past the receptionist at the front door and found our way into Kristine's unguarded coatroom at the top of a staircase. Hanging on the racks was a jungle of fine woolen coats, sleeves sticking out. Hats rested on the shelf above. Some commanders had draped their holstered belts over the hooks as well. It was our great hope that some holsters would still contain German pistols, called Lugers. Two of us took one side of the closet, two the other, thrashing through the heavy wool waistcoats as fast as we could. Every now and then someone would find a gun belt with an empty holster, but success was elusive. The others had already gone back outside when my fingers came to rest around a gleaming black pistol: I was turning it over and over in my hands when I felt someone pushing through the coat sleeves in my direction. I slipped the gun into my pocket and backed out past a German officer with a polite smile and a little bow. I was gone before he could react.

Moments later I was surrounded by the other three Churchill Clubbers out in the street.

"What happened?"

"Only this," I said.

One by one they thrust their hands into my pocket and felt the grand prize. When we got back to the monastery, I tossed the shiny black Luger and two full magazines onto the table.

THE CLUB'S BIGGEST TRIUMPH OF ALL CAME AS A MATTER OF GOOD LUCK AND persistence. One afternoon the boys were riding out by the harbor when Knud noticed two Germans standing on an observation platform and looking out at the harbor through binoculars. About fifty meters behind them was a barracks building with a couple of open windows. Knud skirted behind them and pedaled up close to the building. There, through the open windows, was a machine gun in plain view on a cot. The boys had no automatic weapons, so this would be a new dimension. In many ways the job looked like the rifle heist, but there were important differences.

KNUD PEDERSEN: Even from a distance the machine gun looked way too heavy and bulky to transport on a bike. Also, the two lookout soldiers were dangerously close to the barracks, but at least we could see where they were.

Børge and I returned to the monastery and got a three-wheeled bicycle with a cart on the back. We pedaled it back to the harbor and ditched it as close to the barracks building as we could. Then I went in through the open window and handed the heavy semiautomatic weapon out to Børge. I was about to climb back out when I noticed two canvas bags in the room, one bigger than the other. I figured the heavy one must contain the ammunition, so I passed it out, too, and we took off. We got down to the bottom of a hill, and then we crashed the three-wheeler, spilling the gun onto the road. We looked up behind us, terrified, but the soldiers were still intently focused on the harbor.

We took the stuff to a nearby Boy Scout hut and emptied the contents of the bag. The gun was magnificent, and there were many bullets, but there was one problem: there was no magazine, the chamber that holds a supply of cartridges to be fed automatically to the gun. Without

Stolen machine gun

a magazine the bullets could not be delivered to the weapon and the bloody thing was useless. At our after-school meeting there were howls of laughter.

"Great resistance men you are!"

"Just what we need! A bullet collection!"

But it brought to light once again a naked truth: we had no experience with weapons. Most of us didn't even know what a magazine was. We decided that it was unsafe to go back for the magazine since they'd surely be on the lookout for whoever stole the weapon. We'd have to chalk this up to experience.

But I couldn't stand it. I went back the following day and snatched the other canvas bag, which indeed contained the magazines. There was also a coffee cup in the room that hadn't been there the day before, and a box with the word *Krautkasten* written on it. I figured *Krautkasten* meant "gunpowder" or something. I grabbed it, too, and hauled it back to the monastery. When we pried it open, hearts racing, we found dirty underwear. Krautkasten was the name of the soldier who lived in the room.

By mid-April 1942 the club had amassed an arsenal of knives, bayonets, pistols, rifles, and of course the machine gun. With no military training, and with no one to trust, the boys all struggled to learn to shoot.

KNUD PEDERSEN: Each Sunday morning Jens and I practiced shooting the guns in the gigantic open loft at the top of the monastery during Father's church services. We would lie on our stomachs, waiting for the organ music to swell, and when it did we'd blast away, firing at targets positioned in the hay on the other side of the loft. The machine gun was a Schmeisser, a weapon that German forces had used to shoot thousands of innocent people during the war. It came with a tripod. A setting allowed you to fire one shot at a time, which was helpful in our circumstance, when a hymn could suddenly subside or end altogether.

We never tired of handling the weapons. Several times, shots discharged by accident while we were just messing around in someone's room, nearly ending it all for one or more of us.

Eigil actually put a bullet through his trousers one afternoon in Jens's room. Luckily, the bullet missed his leg, and there was no one from the rest of our family home to hear the explosion.

By the end of April we had about twenty weapons in all, and 432 bullets. We divided up the bullets. I got 112. We always had pistols in our pockets now when we went out on our missions, but these weapons were returned to the monastery at the end of the day. One of our main rules was that no one could take a weapon into the school.

We knew that if police ever caught us with German weapons it would be over. After a while it seemed insane to keep the entire arsenal in one place. We decided to divide the cache, stashing part of it in the monastery and part someplace far away. Helge Milo, who lived in the nearby suburb of Noerresundby, volunteered to keep some of the weapons in his family's garden. It was an appealing idea, except that somehow we would have to transport the weapons across the Limfjorden Bridge with its guard checkpoints at both ends—the one we had crossed to do the Fuchs job at the airport a month or so before.

No one could come up with a better plan. So one evening we packed Helge with weapons from the monastery, taping pistols to his torso and stuffing his clothing with ammunition. When we were done we stood back and looked at him. You could see the outline of a rifle through his trouser leg. The machine gun was under his buttoned jacket, causing him to bend almost double over the handlebars when he got on his bike. The ammunition was concealed in boxes beneath a coat on the luggage rack. It was the best we could do. We posted three Churchill Clubbers on either side of the bridge.

Nervously, we at the monastery pushed Helge off and watched him weave his way toward the bridge, his first wobbly strokes making him look like a child just learning to ride. From time to time he had to get off the bike and walk a few steps with rifle-stiffened legs. It was clumsy for him to reboard. This didn't look good. What would happen when he got to the heavily guarded bridge? What if he was asked for an identity card and searched? Somehow, he cleared the first checkpoint. The three Clubbers awaiting him at the Noerresundby side at first mocked his hunched-over posture and stiff leg as he approached, but their laughter died quickly as they, too, realized this was a serious and perhaps decisive matter.

The Churchill Club trios at both ends of the Limfjorden Bridge held their collective breath as our comrade Helge, packing hard-won assets, tottered up to the second guard station on the far side, paused, and was waved on through. Somehow he had made it!

Drawing by Knud of art supplies that cluttered his room at Holy Ghost Monastery

8

An Evening Alone

KNUD PEDERSEN: ONE NIGHT AFTER AN ESPECIALLY RAUCOUS CHURCHILL Club meeting I sat in my room with the door shut and tried to stop my head from spinning. It was amazing how suddenly the old monastery could go from bedlam to silence when the last member pulled the door shut behind him. I rubbed my hands together to keep warm. There wasn't enough coal in Denmark to heat this place.

I looked around my room. My living space was actually more a studio than a room. Canvases were stacked in corners, and sketches were strewn all over the floor. Paintbrushes protruded from cloudy water in jars that occupied nearly every flat space. I painted the way other guys played sports. Landscapes and portraits and abstractions covered my walls, the ceiling, even the window curtains. I had painted half a scene on my desk—now I realized I had never completed it.

My parents saved money to send Jens—the family golden boy—off to college. And who could blame them? Jens was already respected as the best math student at Cathedral School. But my parents did something special for me as well. When we moved to Aalborg, Father opened up an account in my name at the local art store. I could purchase all the brushes and easels and tubes of paint I wanted. And as a result I could hardly make my way around this little room without putting a shoe through a canvas or knocking over a jar.

But tonight I didn't even feel like painting. There was too much to think about. War shadowed everything. I pulled the window curtain back: What were all those cars doing at Budolfi Square? The lines of vehicles kept getting longer and longer. Would they soon be on a transport ship to Norway, and then on another to cross the North Sea? Were the Germans staging to invade England? I glared at the German soldier guarding the post office. He shared a round-the-clock shift with two other soldiers. I could see one of them every time I looked outside.

My mind drifted: What would my life be like if Germany won? If Hitler had his way we'd be part of an *Überreich*, held up to the world as a master race, with defeated people forced to work as slaves to satisfy their masters. If the bloody Nazis won, the Churchill Club, or something like us, would have to move even further underground. Someone would have to keep hope alive. We would be forced to continue resisting in an occupied country after the war.

I wished I had someone to talk with about all this. Sure, Jens was my brother and he shared the danger of our work, but he wasn't someone I could confide in. We competed over everything. It could get ridiculous. Back in Odense we both fell in love with the American movie star Deanna Durbin. We had one photo of her and we tore it in half so that neither of us could have her to himself. Same thing with our record player, a gramophone. It had a detachable crank arm that you had to use to get it started. I would take the record of Deanna Durbin singing,

Deanna Durbin

72

and Jens would grab the arm. We could only hear her when we were together—the last place we wanted to be.

Børge shared my sense of humor, but he was too young and didn't go to my school. And I was not all that close to the others in the Churchill Club, even though most were in my grade. We shared a common passion to awaken Denmark—that was enough.

No, I wanted to open my heart to a particular someone special. Grethe Rørbæk was a student in the ninth grade, like me. Tall and blond, she wore no makeup but had a natural beauty and a wonderful smile. Though she was in my grade, I had no classes with her—she was in the advanced classes; I was in the B group. The closest we ever came to exchanging a word was a magical day we crossed paths in the yard between classes. She had a box of small sandwiches and stopped to offer me one. I couldn't say a word. In fact, I was so flustered I didn't even return to school that day. I walked home and lay down on the couch in Father's office. Mother—without asking questions—served me warm tea and stayed with me.

My shyness didn't stop me from having heroic fantasies starring the two of us. One was set in Budolfi Square. The Churchill Club had climbed to the top of the church tower and we were hurling mortar shells and bombs onto the square below. Flames erupted from the German vehicles, one car setting the next ablaze in a furious chain of pyrotechnics. In the most glorious moment, I drove into the square in a small, open car. I stood up in the car with one foot on the seat, waving a pistol with my free hand. By now the square was an inferno. Bombs and exploding engines threw sheets of brilliant light, illuminating charred, frightened faces peering out from the shadows. I drove on through a hail of bullets. And suddenly, over the whine of lead, I heard a scream from the top floor of a building on the square. I looked up and there was Grethe, standing, eyes wide, her sweet hands pressed to her mouth, her slender form illuminated by fire. We locked eyes meaningfully, and then I lost sight of her.

The fantasy usually popped about then, crushed beneath the weight of its own absurdity. The pitiful truth was, I had never had a serious conversation with any girl, not even my sister, Gertrud. When I first got to

Cathedral School, I tried to impress girls by getting in fights. That's the way you had gained status in my old school at Odense. But that had been an all-boys school, where you settled everything with your fists behind the school by the statue of the businessman Carl Frederik Tietgen. Now, I'd knock somebody down and look around and see girls backing away. They seemed horrified, not impressed. Finally, somebody convinced me I'd do better with girls by opening doors for them and inviting them to precede me in line, or figuring out how to help them with their coats. So far, nearly one semester into Cathedral School, that hadn't worked any better. I was still light-years away from kissing my first girl, with no candidates on the horizon.

There was just so much to think about. We of the Churchill Club were brave but naïve and undisciplined. Just days before, at a skating rink, Jens had skated up behind a German soldier and kicked him in the leg. The guy howled in pain and took off after Jens, who was chased down and taken to the police station. Now his name was enshrined in a registry of those who opposed the Nazis. Just what we needed.

And it was only by the greatest good fortune that Helge had made it over the Limfjorden Bridge with our weapons, now buried in his garden. Had we taken too great a risk? There were so many near misses. What if the German soldier washing the windows had turned around to see me making off with the rifle? Would I have had to shoot him? Would I have known how? Was the rifle even loaded? What if the woman on the street had yelled for the police as we pedaled away? What if the German officer at Kristine had moved his body to block my way out of the coat closet?

But there were even more ominous thoughts crowding my brain for headline space as I tried to relax in my room. Eigil's older sister was a secretary with the Aalborg police. She was the only outsider who knew about us, and it was good to have a trusted mole embedded with the authorities. However, her news wasn't good. The German command had issued an ultimatum to Danish police: either you identify and arrest whoever has been damaging our property and stealing our weapons, or we'll find them ourselves, with drastic results for the criminals. If this continues, they were saying, Germany's infamous secret state police force, the Gestapo, will take over the policing of Aalborg.

Eigil's sister said that two elite professional investigators had been sent up from Copenhagen and were now drawing closer every day. A witness from Café Holle—where we had lifted a German pistol—and two fishermen who had seen us steal weapons at the waterfront were directing investigators toward Cathedral School.

Stop now, Eigil's sister pleaded; lie low. She and her brother had a very strong personal interest at stake: theirs was the only Jewish family among the Churchill Club members. Eigil feared that his arrest could lead to capture by the Nazis and death for his entire family. Overnight, Eigil had suddenly gone from pushing us to go out on missions every day to begging us to close down. His nerves were raw and his emotions very turbulent.

Lying low was the last thing I wanted. Norwegians were still fighting and dying, and Danes were still singing folk songs and buying King's Badges. We were still occupied. The Germans seemed more at home in Aalborg by the day. If I had to go down, I wanted to go down fighting like the hero of my fantasies.

Flames flickered from the tiny stove in my room at the monastery. The German guard outside my window kept pacing robotically, back and forth, and finally, many hours after our meeting had concluded, I fell asleep.

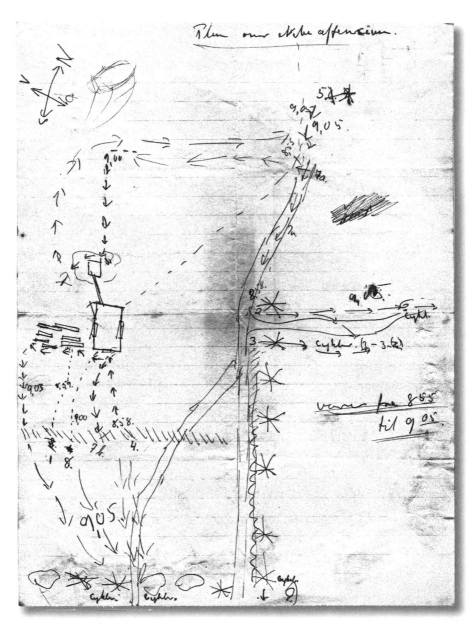

Knud's diagram of the plan for the Nibe attack

9

The Nibe Offensive

EARLY IN MAY 1942, BØRGE DECIDED ON HIS OWN TO TRY OUT A NEW RECRUIT for the Churchill Club. Perhaps he had visions of starting his own club; his motive was never clear to the others. The candidate was a friend from Nibe, the small town outside of Aalborg where Børge lived. He gave this boy, who was only thirteen, a can of blue paint and told him to go paint the club's insignia—the swastika with arrows proclaiming the rebellion against the Nazis—all over town. But Nibe was a close-knit community in which everybody knew each other. Within minutes the boy was in police custody, getting his ears boxed by an officer who warned him to forget his childish fantasies of revolution. The officer gave the boy a wire brush and a bucket of suds and ordered him to get busy removing the paint from all the walls he had defaced.

As he scrubbed the boy became angrier and angrier. By the time he was finished he had conceived a plan. He told Børge of a remote German guard post, an armed tower in the sand dunes on the outskirts of town. It had a searchlight that swept back and forth for great distances to give the Germans a view out over the North Sea toward England. The post was manned by three German soldiers who lived together in a nearby barracks.

The angry boy proposed to use the Churchill Club's weapons to kill the German soldiers. The Nibe offensive—as he called it—would show the world who was a child and who meant business. Intrigued, Børge went to Aalborg to try the proposal out on the rest of the Churchill Club.

KNUD PEDERSEN: When our anger at Børge for trying out a new recruit without telling us—"What were you thinking!?"—subsided, we coldly considered the proposal to shoot the German guards at Nibe. It wasn't the first time the club had mulled over a killing. Weeks before, another member had advocated stabbing a German guard in the back, but he was shouted down by others who said such an act would violate our code of fair play: An enemy must have a chance.

On the one hand, this idea of Børge's was the same sort of thing—a sneak attack. And it also violated a second key club proposition: Never kill for personal revenge. But on the other hand, the club's mission included a vow to minimize the Germans who had stolen our country. How could one minimize them more than by *erasing* them? Besides, now we had weapons. Were we ever going to use them, or did we just intend to let them rust in Helge's parsley garden and the monastery cellar until the British came to liberate us?

The motion for the Nibe offensive was raised, and the action was approved by the members. I helped Børge draw up an attack diagram, but I refused to go with him. I did not favor his mission. Besides, we had an action planned in Aalborg at the railway yard for the same evening—a military-style attack that would use our new weapons. I told Børge our strike was much more important than biking out to Nibe to quench some boy's bloodlust. But Børge had his mind made up. I didn't waste time trying to dissuade him.

BØRGE LATER TOLD KNUD THAT HE TOOK OFF FOR NIBE WITH TWO COMPANIONS, one the angry boy and the other a Churchill Club regular who volunteered

German anti-aircraft gun position, 1940, with a Danish farmer tilling his field in the foreground

to go. They stopped at Helge's garden to pick up the machine gun and a pair of pistols, then continued on.

The boys arrived at Nibe in the early afternoon. They stashed their weapons in a nearby Boy Scout hut and took a reconnaissance walk along the dunes in the late afternoon. They strolled up the hill toward the German barracks. Suddenly the door kicked open from the inside and one of the German soldiers appeared, not in a crisp military uniform, but in shirtsleeves and suspenders, smoking his pipe. He was quickly joined by his mates. The three jolly soldiers saluted the kids, wished them a good afternoon, and waved them to come up. The group stood outside in the sunshine and had a cordial conversation. These guys clearly didn't get much company way out there, and they were happy to see the boys. They talked about their grandchildren back in Germany. It got harder and harder to view them as part of Hitler's deadly Wehrmacht. By the time he got back to the hut, Børge was deeply conflicted. Why kill these three grandfathers?

Is that really the war he wanted to fight? But they were on a mission to take out these particular German guards. They'd been authorized to do it, and now they were duty-bound. A mission was a mission.

When darkness fell they carried their weapons to a drainage ditch at the bottom of a grassy hill below the German barracks. They spread out into three columns—Børge front and center with the machine gun, and the other two flanking him with pistols. The plan was to crawl through the grass on their bellies up the hill. When they got close enough, they would pause. Then on a time count they would smash through the door and open fire.

As they slithered through the wet grass, Børge tried to put himself in the mind-set of a warrior. This was necessary, he reminded himself. This would show the Germans what April 9 was all about. This would wake up the docile Danes. He could see the newspaper headline: "Germans Shot Down with Their Own Weapons by Young Boys!" The light from a single candle inside the barracks danced with every step closer. Thirty meters from the structure, there was still no sound. Børge's hands were trembling. And then, suddenly, the door opened. One of the old men came out on the porch and looked around. Had he heard something?

The soldier stood for a while, then closed the door behind him, walked across the dune grass to the guard station, and climbed up the ladder to his listening post. Now the target was spread out—two Germans in one building, one in another. All three were above them. The boys' chances of mission success had just plummeted. Now it looked more like a suicide mission than a carefully conceived assault.

Their thoughts swiftly turned from murder to escape. They lay motionless for what felt like hours, pressed down flat in the grass. They were wet, cold, and terrified. The German up in his listening post at the lighthouse surely had a rifle. After a time they began to inch backward down through the grass, bodies cramped with tension. It took nearly a half hour to reach the ditch, and longer to creep back to their hut. Once safely inside, the boys attacked one another verbally, each blaming the others for chickening out.

Exhausted and humiliated, Børge stormed out of the hut and took off on his bike, leaving the others behind. He dreaded telling the rest of the Churchill Club of the Nibe offensive's failure—but more than that he hungered to be part of the night's activities in Aalborg. Børge sped fifteen miles through the dark countryside hoping to reach the Aalborg railway yard in time to take part in what promised to be the Churchill Club's biggest and most daring action yet.

Police photo of railroad freight car targeted by the Churchill Club

10

Grenades

THOUGH THE WEHRMACHT'S HOBNAILED BOOTS ECHOED THROUGH AALBORG'S streets, though a blue cloud of gasoline and oil from German transport wagons hung over the city, though Eigil's sister insisted that detectives were but a breath away from the Churchill Club—it was still spring. The air had warmed, and the days were long and bright at last. The oldest Cathedral School students were just a few days from graduation. Helge, Eigil, Knud, and the Professor would be moving into high school at last—if they could pass their finals. The young saboteurs kept up their resistance work even as they crammed for exams. Classmates had no clue what was going on. Instructors constantly reminded students that they were growing in experience and responsibility. The instructors had no idea how right they were—at least for a few of them.

A bright spot was that the Churchill Club suddenly acquired three important new allies, thanks to Uffe Darket. Every few evenings Uffe rode his bike downtown to attend meetings of a model-airplane-building hobby club. One night as he carved his parts and glued them together, Uffe fell into conversation with another plane builder named Alf Houlberg. Alf, his brother Kaj, and their friend Knud Hornbo were in their early twenties, factory workers from the nearby town of Brønderslev. They all were devoted to model airplanes.

They kept chatting as they worked, until, after a time, Uffe took a chance and revealed his activities with the Churchill Club to Alf. Far from being shocked, Alf replied that the three of them shared Uffe's disgust with the Danish authorities in this crisis. In fact, they had just stolen six mortar grenades from the railway station near their factory. Problem was, they couldn't figure out how to make the bloody things work. Would the Churchill Club be able to use them?

KNUD PEDERSEN: My brother brought the mortar rounds to the monastery in two heavy cases Uffe had given him. He was carrying them very carefully. The only thing I had ever heard about mortar grenades was that they exploded on contact. I told Jens to set them down on the bed gently. He accidentally nicked the bedpost with one of them, and our hearts about stopped. We lifted the lids. Inside each box were three objects that looked like iron bowling pins with wire caps smeared with fat. As usual, we didn't know how to operate them. And as always, there was no one to teach us.

Jens and the Professor immediately started to tinker with them in the Professor's lab above Jens's room. Their first idea was to take one of the grenades apart on a table and empty the explosive powder from it. But when they got the parts all spread out, they found that there was no powder inside. It was puzzling: the only thing we could figure was that Alf and his mates must have stolen practice grenades: dummies, not live munitions. The Professor and Jens resumed experimenting with the grenade components, inspecting them, combining them, turning them over and over, trying to make *something* happen. Then at the bottom of the grenade they found something interesting: a thin metal disc of seven or eight centimeters, held in place by a set of screws. Something about that disc just *looked* flammable.

A match to the disc lit the Professor's lab up like seven suns! They were yelling bloody murder, and the rest of us came running in with water. It took at least a minute to extinguish the flames. Through the heavy smoke the two great scientists were grinning like the triumphant fools they were.

The two kept working. They came to realize that the discs themselves were made of highly flammable magnesium. All they had to do was light one with a match and they had a compact firebomb. I don't know how we lived through those tests: Jens and the Professor were world champions in near-suicidal experiments with explosives, but this time they figured out how to control the materials. At last the Professor had made a weapon that worked.

It was a big step, for grenades brought powerful dreams within reach. Now we could stage raids of our own.

We set aside two grenades for our ultimate mission: destroying the German vehicles that lined the streets of Budolfi Square outside my window. At last we had the force to make it happen—well, maybe not exactly like my fantasy, where I came racing into the square with guns blazing and caught sight of Grethe in the tower, but at least the Nazi-fighting heart of it. Now we had the firepower to mount a serious assault.

But first a field test.

When darkness fell on the evening of May 2, 1942, five of us biked to the Aalborg rail yards, a hub of Nazi activity in Aalborg. It was a city of boxcars, lined up in rusted strings. Some containers were filled with ore from Norway and Sweden. Others were loaded with machine parts and components. Still others contained materials for the rapidly expanding Aalborg airport. The yard, lit with floodlights, screeched with the clamor of groaning engines and banging doors and wheels scraping on iron rails. Tonight's mission was to use our new grenades to ignite boxcars and destroy their contents. We had high hopes.

A chain-link fence patrolled by two armed guards kept the public away from the rail yard. A footpath ran in front of the fence. One of us would remain on the path as a sentry, chatting with the guards if necessary, clanging an alarm on a metal fence post if something went wrong. The others would cut a hole in the fence and enter the yard. Alf and Uffe would take positions beneath boxcars, each with a pistol trained on a guard. I and one other would go to work on the freight cars with the grenades.

As we crept toward the fence we met a problem we hadn't counted on. A pair of lovers had positioned themselves at one end of the path and were furiously making out. How could we flush them out without explaining why we wanted them to leave? We moved up close and stared, eyes wide, mimicking them. With middle fingers raised in farewell, they left for a more private place.

We cut the fence and took our positions. Uffe slid underneath a boxcar and aimed his pistol at a guard. Another Clubber and I set to work picking out a likely boxcar to ignite. We walked to the middle of a train, figuring it would be harder for Germans to extract a flaming boxcar from the middle than to just uncouple one at the front or back.

The first rusty old iron door screamed when I pulled it back. My eyes adjusted, and yes! It was full of airplane wings! Better still, there were paper drawings showing how to attach the wings to the fuselage of a plane. It was a jackpot target of tremendous value to the Nazis.

I bunched up a pile of wing-assembly instructions and gingerly placed a grenade disc atop the pyre. Crouching in the doorway, I lit a match and tossed it backward onto the pile of paper. The flames ignited the disk quicker than I anticipated, and the explosion of fire hit me in midflight as I leaped from the boxcar. Flames were already consuming the paper and wings when I landed on the ground. My partner did the same to the next boxcar, and we ran crouching toward the fence. I whistled that the operation was complete, and we all squirmed back through the hole we'd cut in the fence.

Just about that time, Børge came huffing in from Nibe on his bicycle, hours after his failed offensive. He was just in time to admire our work. We all backed into the darkness and watched events play out. Sirens began to scream throughout the city. Then German officers rushed past us toward the rail yard. There was a wild arm-waving discussion between the arriving Danish firemen and the German officers. At first the Danes refused to go into the area because they feared some of those boxcars contained live ammunition. The Germans, hands on pistols, insisted.

Danish firemen started rolling out their hoses, but they moved very slowly, sometimes standing on the hoses once water began to flow. Brandishing their pistols, the Germans shouted at them to *move,* but it was obvious that the firemen were stalling to let the fire take hold and damage the Third Reich's treasure. This moment was significant to us: Danish authorities—the firemen—were standing up to German orders. For the first time in a long while we felt a stirring of pride in our countrymen.

It was our biggest success so far, the destruction of a major German asset. This was the closest we had come yet to a military-style action, one in which we were well armed and had a deployment strategy. It was satisfying to stand there seeing flames lick the night and to witness the discomfort it caused the scrambling Germans. But if we had known what was about to come, we would not have been standing around admiring our work.

We would already have been in motion.

A portion of the Churchill Club's weapons cache, including the six mortar grenades

11

No Turning Back

KNUD PEDERSEN: DURING THE ENTIRE FIRST WEEK OF MAY 1942, OUR NERVES were stretched taut. We were elated that we had pulled off the rail yard action, but anxiety mounted as Eigil's sister warned us that the special security police had identified Cathedral School as the hub of sabotage activity in Aalborg. Now we glanced around anxiously wherever we went. We felt, or imagined, eyes upon us everywhere. We heard footsteps. We lived in an atmosphere of fear.

All the tension boiled over one afternoon in Jens's study. Eigil demanded through tears that we cease sabotage activity altogether. He accused us all of risking the lives of his family, since his mother was Jewish. Hitler would stop at nothing to erase the Jewish population. We would feel the same way, he insisted, if we were in his shoes. Jens was moved to support him. Børge and I would hear none of it. We were single-minded. Nothing has changed, we said. Danes are still lapdogs. Germans are still swine. Norwegians still resist. So, therefore, will we. We will never turn back. Enough of this: let us return our attention to the Nazi roadsters lined outside the post office on Budolfi Square.

While bright birds sang cheerfully and flowers burst into bloom outside our windows, we stayed inside and tore ourselves apart that afternoon. The club was deeply and bitterly divided. Jens and I nearly came to blows and had to be held apart. Finally, I stormed out with Børge beside me, slamming the door behind us. Jens and the others stayed behind.

About five o'clock on the afternoon of May 6, waitress Elsa Ottesen at Café Holle in downtown Aalborg saw two teenage boys enter the restaurant, walking briskly. Heads down, they made a beeline for the coat closet and emerged from it a very short time later. They strode straight out of the restaurant without ordering a thing. Looking through the café's picture window, Mrs. Ottesen saw them talking on the street.

A few minutes later a German officer dining at the café discovered that his gun was missing. He had placed his belt and holster—with the pistol inside—on a shelf in the café's coat closet. After his meal, he went to recover his sidearm and found that the holster was empty. He angrily reported this misfortune to the full restaurant staff, which sparked Mrs. Ottesen's memory of the two boys who entered the coat closet.

Mrs. Ottesen gave a detailed statement to police. Yes, she'd seen these boys before. They had been in the restaurant a few times, always preoccupied with the coat closet, never ordering. Several times she'd seen them clustered around their bicycles out in front of the café, talking. At least twice she'd seen them peering through their framed fingers into the café window. One of them—very tall—combed his thick hair with a dramatic upsweep. She thought she could recognize him if she saw him again.

KNUD PEDERSEN: School let out at three on Friday, May 8. Another week down, just a few days left till summer break. I was walking out through the school gate with Helge, jabbering about something when I caught sight of a sharply dressed gentleman across the street with a lady at his side. Both seemed to be staring straight at us. I had never seen them before, but their eyes never left us. To create a distraction while I got a better look at them, I pulled my long black comb from my pocket and swept it up through my hair. It was the kiss of death. "It's him," Mrs. Elsa Ottesen no doubt said to her companion. "The tall one."

I said to Helge, "See that guy in a suit we just passed? He's following us. Don't look back. Let's stop for a minute." We stopped. They stopped, too, the man staring intently through a grocery store window as though turnips were all that mattered in the world. We sprinted around a corner and stopped again. Moments later, the man came skidding around the same corner and nearly crashed into us. "Security Police!" the man barked. "May I see your identification cards?" It was an order, not a request.

Hours later, the front doorbell rang at the monastery. When our maid opened it a crack, police shouldered through and bulled straight into Jens's room, shouting that he was under arrest. Jens had a fully loaded pistol in his desk drawer but wisely kept his hands away from it.

"Where are the weapons?" the officers demanded. Jens stood up and led them straight to the cellar to our secret weapons cache.

By midnight they had us all. Eleven were arrested, six from Cathedral School, plus Børge and Uffe from other schools. Børge was soon separated from us because, at fourteen, he was too young to be imprisoned under Danish law. They also nabbed Alf and Kaj Houlberg and Knud Hornbo, the three older factory workers from Brønderslev who had given us the mortar grenades. Police separated us and interviewed us one at a time at the Aalborg police station. Soon every room was chattering with the sound of Remington typewriters taking down the testimony of boys lying through their teeth. The police got ever angrier as they tore paper from the rolls, wadded it up, and threatened the suspects with harsher punishment if they continued to lie.

Two cops—the two detectives from Copenhagen—led me into an office, pointed to a chair, and shut the door. The subject on their mind was grenades. Where did we get them?

"Well," I said, "I met a fellow during intermission at the movies. He happened to mention that he had some grenades, and I asked if we could use them."

"What was his name?"

"He didn't mention his name."

One of them came across the room, took me up by my shoulders and slammed me into a wall. "Your father is a priest!" he shouted, his beet-red face no more than two inches from mine. "He tells you it is a sin to lie! And you are *lying* to me! Now, you tell me, boy . . . what is the name of the person who gave you the grenades?"

I insisted I didn't know.

"Well, then, what did he look like?"

I told them—brown curly hair and brown eyes. And that's all I gave them about Alf, one tiny little fact. When we were finished I was feeling pretty good about myself—I had held my tongue under fierce questioning. Of course the investigators went to the next captive and asked, "What is the name of the guy with the brown curly hair who gave you grenades?"

"Alf," said someone.

And so on. Soon, working one boy against another, interviewing them alone, they had Alf and Kaj's last name, and Knud Hornbo's as well. We were interviewed so professionally that we gave them information even as we thought we were cleverly concealing it. Also, our stories kept crossing and it was impossible to keep lying.

THE BOYS' PARENTS BEGAN TO ARRIVE IN THE EARLY EVENING. SOME HAD BEEN home when police burst in and hauled their boys brusquely away. Others were just now finding out and racing, panic-stricken and confused, to the station. They were received by the police commissioner, an elderly white-haired man named C. L. Bach. Tears of sympathy filled his eyes as he escorted each set of parents to his office and did his best to explain.

KNUD PEDERSEN: Our parents were mute, speechless, shocked. None of them knew a thing about the Churchill Club and our activities. Their eyes widened as the commissioner told them what their supposedly bridge-playing sons had really been doing over the past six months. And the parents did not know each other, which only added to the strangeness of the atmosphere. Some of them—factory owners, doctors, lawyers, the most prominent figures of the city—had never been in a police station before.

My parents bustled into the station formally dressed from a wedding, Mother with her pearls and Father in his tuxedo. They had been summoned to a phone at the wedding and, when informed that their sons had been arrested, had made it to the police station within five minutes. Though Jens and I were proud of what we had done—standing up for our country—it was hard to look our parents in the eyes that night. Some parents repeated again and again, "How *could* you?" But not ours. They cared first and foremost that we were safe and that we had not been treated roughly in the arrest. Jens and I didn't expect that our parents would reprove or punish us for what we had done. They were activists, public people, community leaders who viewed this family misfortune as just one more example of the unhappiness that war brings. As the saying goes, "In peacetime, the children bury their parents. In wartime, the parents bury their children." Surely they were proud of us.

Police questioned us all through the night. It was amazing how much information the offer of a single cigarette could produce at midnight when you had been smokeless all day long. At two in the morning, the police were finally satisfied. There were some actions that we managed to keep hidden, but they got most of it out of us. Each boy had to sign a written statement. Still cocky, though we could barely hold our heads up, some of us signed with artistic flourishes that swept up over our names.

Finally just before dawn we were herded into a police van with armed guards and transported to the King Hans Gades Jail—Aalborg's city jail— where we turned in our belongings and were locked into cells. We were given prison gowns and told to place our clothes on a chair outside the cell. My cellmate was Jens. As soon as the guard went away we went to the window and tried the bars. Thick, square, and solidly rooted they were. I lay down on a mattress and my eyes soon closed. It would be a long time before I slept as a free man again.

Photograph posed for Hitler in the yard of King Hans Gades Jail: Knud (1), Jens (2), Mogens F. (3), Eigil (4), Helge (5), Uffe (6), Mogens T. (7), Børge (no number); man at right unknown

12

King Hans Gades Jail

KNUD PEDERSEN: A VERY FEW HOURS LATER I WAS JOLTED AWAKE BY THE voice of a guard. "Put on your clothes. You are going to court! Now."

I rubbed my eyes and looked around. Jens had grabbed the only bed; I had fallen asleep on a floor mattress. Pale light filtered in through a barred window high in one of the four walls. At the other end of our small, oblong cell was a solid door with no handle and a peephole covered on the outside—so that the guards could check on us but we couldn't see out. A table and a stool were bolted to the linoleum floor. That was it. Home.

We were transported to court by bus with Danish uniformed police guards, one guard for each of us. Outside the bus window the streets were filled with people bustling to work and school as usual, except, of course, that under German occupation they were no freer than we were.

The courtroom was a solemn square chamber with high windows and a polished linoleum floor. It took only a few minutes for the judge, barely looking up from his papers, to extend our confinement by four weeks and send us back to our cells.

• • •

As Knud and the others were being transported to and from court, Rector Kjeld Galster, the Cathedral School principal, stood before the students at morning assembly and informed them that six of their classmates had been arrested overnight and charged with sabotage against the German Army. He read their names out: Knud Pedersen. Jens Pedersen. Eigil Astrup-Frederiksen. Helge Milo. Mogens Fjellerup. Mogens Thomsen. Your classmates, he said, are now behind bars at King Hans Gades Jail.

Cathedral School principal, Rector Kjeld Galster

Some students rose from their seats and ran out of the building. Teachers stood aside. Students massed outside the jail chanting and cheering for their classmates.

The boys, in court, did not hear them.

Other students remained at school, deeply shaken. One later wrote, "The announcement was completely shocking to us. These six guys who, as late as the day before yesterday had walked among us at school, learned their lessons with us, and played with us on the school grounds, had in their nonschool time made sabotage against the Germans . . . The rector urged us to go to our classes and resume our work. But it was hard . . . We developed a gruesome picture of the fate our companions would share. We sat and looked across the empty benches where our arrested comrades used to sit. One of our teachers sat for an hour with his head buried in his hands and did not say a word to us."

Another Cathedral teacher found something constructive to do with the powerful feelings that seized him when he heard the news. It was Knud's shop teacher. He knew that Knud hated shop class and had no interest in woodworking. For almost a semester now he had yelled at Knud, berating him as lazy, calling him inept in front of the other students. Regret overwhelmed him. Out of deep admiration for what the boy had been doing, he set to work on finishing Knud's class project. And when he was finished, he delivered a finely crafted table to the monastery and left it as a gift for the Pedersen family.

WORD OF THE SABOTAGE CELL AND THE BOYS' ARREST SWEPT QUICKLY THROUGH the city of Aalborg.

Gossip raged in shops, offices, schools, and factories.

Behind the scenes, German and Danish officials were already engaged in tense negotiations. These were the first sabotage arrests in Denmark during the war—all eyes would be on this case. The big question was: Who would conduct the trial, Denmark or Germany? If the boys were convicted, under which system of justice would they be punished? If German authorities issued the sentences, the boys could wind up in pitiless work camps at best. At worst, should Hitler decide to treat them as public examples of what happened to people who dared to resist, they could be executed. If the Churchill Club was tried in Danish court, the Danes' German masters would surely insist on quick convictions and harsh sentences to show the world that the Third Reich meant business.

And there was something else at stake: the deal between Germany and Denmark. Many Danes were content with the occupation. Money was being made; their homes were still standing. For their part, German soldiers and officers were well fed, had the run of Denmark's cities, and barely had to lift a finger to preserve the status quo. No troops were needed to police the Danes; the mere threat of German military might kept them in line. For many on both sides it was a sweet arrangement. But these boys had stirred things up, and how they were handled was important. On the one hand, the Germans did not want to arouse public anger by crushing these Danish youths, but on the other hand, they couldn't appear to be weak either. It was a very delicate situation.

Three days after the boys were arrested, the Aalborg City Council delivered a contrite letter to German authorities apologizing for the Churchill Club's behavior. Signed by the mayor, it said:

> Aalborg City Council has unfortunately received word that a number of young people who are pupils at the Cathedral School . . . have undertaken varying and extremely serious harassment of the German Army . . . On behalf of the people of the city, the City Council expresses deep regret . . . concerning these actions. This has given rise to sorrow and dismay in many homes, which—the council has been assured—had no idea of the illegal actions which have taken place. The City Council furthermore expresses their hope that what has taken place will not lead to serious consequences for the continuation of the good relationship between the German Army and the Danish State and Council Authorities.

In the end, Germany allowed Denmark to conduct the trial, but with conditions. First, the Germans insisted that Rector Galster be removed as head of Cathedral School and banished from Aalborg. Second, the occupiers made it clear that during the trial a German observer would be in the courtroom at all times, watching carefully and reporting to Berlin. A judge and a prosecutor were summoned to Aalborg from the nation's capital, Copenhagen, to conduct the trial of the Churchill Club.

KNUD PEDERSEN: In jail we were treated differently from other prisoners. For one thing we *were* different from other prisoners—a pack of teenage boys from a private school. The police were used to drunks and thieves. Beyond that, we were behind bars for actions that some of our jailers deeply admired. We were star prisoners, receiving the best treatment our jailers could give us. Kristine, the pastry shop from which we had stolen three pistols, sent coffee over to us. Even Holle's, the café whose waitress had ratted us out, started sending over cream cakes for us. And, even though we were in deep trouble, we had the cheer and energy of teens everywhere. We made the best of our situation. And we were deeply, to the core, irreverent.

From time to time we were taken to see a doctor assigned to assess our mental health. It would have been convenient for Danish officials to report that tests indicated that insanity had driven us to sabotage. Our doctor looked deep into our eyes and asked such questions as "If I gave you ten thousand kroner, how would you spend it?" Alf told me he answered by saying, "Thank you, but that's too much money. I'd feel better with five thousand."

The doctor gave us written exams to test our general knowledge:

"Why do the seasons change between summer and winter?"
"When did Queen Elizabeth reign?"
"What is the capital of Portugal?"
"What is gratitude?"

Now that last question was interesting. One of us answered with "If I get ten years and stand up and say 'Thank you,' that will be gratitude."

We were permitted an hour outside in the prison yard every day. We would be in our cells reading and writing, or building model airplanes, or trying to sleep, when keys would rattle in the door and a jailer would shout, "Recreation time!" We were led into one of two cement dungeons with walls about ten feet high and mesh netting over the top. Some of us played chess, others played ball games. Once when we heard German soldiers tromping outside the walls, bleating one of their stupid farm ballads, we quickly countered with "It's a Long Way to Tipperary," the marching song made famous by British soldiers during the First World War. The Germans complained to the prison authorities.

We wrote a letter to the police commissioner, seeking permission to smoke during outdoor time. "We ask you, dear commissioner, to let us smoke a single cigarette," we wrote. "We promise to stub it out and promise not to take it into the cell. We guarantee you this promise will be kept." We all signed it. And it worked!

Every day we made up plays and skits that mocked the authorities. We played trial scenes over and over in the jail yard, imitating the court

Hr. Politimester.

Hermed tillader vi os at forespørge Hr. Politimesteren om De ikke vil give os Lov til at ryge en enkelt Cigaret paa Gaardturen.

Vi lover allesammen at slukke den og lade være med at tage den med ind i Arresten. Vi indestaar for at dette Løfte vil blive holdt

Ærbødigst

Jens Bue Pedersen   Knud Pedersen.
ay Hauberg.   Mogens Fjellerup.
K. Hauberg.   K. Kornbo
Mogens Thomsen   Uffe Darket
Eigil Astrup-Frederiksen
        Helge Milo.

Letter to the Aalborg police commissioner seeking permission to smoke a cigarette during outdoor time

officials we were coming to know. The plays always ended with the death penalty to all of us—we put a white hanky over our hearts when we died— and, no doubt about it, we were deeply worried about being executed. We spent a lot of time discussing how they would do it. Shoot us? If so, all at once in a row or one by one? Would it hurt? For how long? Someone had seen a movie where Nazi-like thugs had executed a bunch of prisoners. The goons used the same shirt, which had a hole in the heart, and put it on each new prisoner to be shot so they wouldn't have to dirty a new shirt each time. At King Hans Gades Jail we had one cell containing an older prisoner, a guy who said he had murdered his wife when he found out she was a Nazi. This guy pretended he knew everything about everything. He said he had heard that the suffering from execution could last for a half hour.

Each of us handled confinement differently. I was all nervous energy. I made a clutter of everything, strewing drawings all over the cell, while Jens was tidy by nature. This had been okay when we lived in separate rooms in the monastery, but now we were thrown together twenty-three hours a day in a tiny cell. For a while he blocked me out as best he could, trying to concentrate on reading *The Brothers Karamazov*. But one day he scowled over the book and told me to shut up. Soon we were nose to nose, voices rising as we blamed each other for doing things that got us all arrested.

> Jens: Why did you tell the police about the three guys from Brønderslev who gave us the grenades? You didn't have to. We could have saved them!
>
> Me: I *had* to explain the grenades because *you* led police straight to our stash in the cellar.
>
> Jens: I didn't show them the cellar. *You* told them about it.
>
> Me: All I told them was that you were my brother. And why did it even come up? Because *you* had the brains to trip a German skater on an ice rink and get yourself on an anti-Nazi watch list. What an idiot you are!
>
> Jens: Bloody Nazi!
>
> Me: Bloody Communist!

Then we were swinging, two brothers who loved each other but who had been in a pressure cooker for more than half a year. All the Churchill Club meetings were at our home. All roads led to us. It just got to be too much, and it all came pouring out that afternoon.

Everyone in the prison started yelling, and guards rushed in to separate us. They put Jens in the cell next door, locked in with Alf. There were sore feelings as we went to bed that evening, but in the end this arrangement allowed us to combine our talents productively.

One day the guards summoned us to the prison yard for a photograph. We were surprised to see Børge again, the first time since the night of our arrest. He had been arrested like all of us, but was too young to be charged as an adult. He said he was spending his time in a youth correctional facility. We were each given a number to hold up in front of us and told to spread out side by side. We started to make fun of the whole thing as usual, but a guard brought us up short: "You'd better look as serious and sad as you can," he said, "because these photos are going straight to Berlin. Hitler himself may see them. You would be very wise to wipe those smiles off your faces." And we did. And suddenly Børge's appearance made sense. As the youngest and most innocent-looking of us, he helped make the impression, one that Danish officials desperately sought to convey, that we were just innocent schoolkids who had been caught on a lark.

KNUD AND HIS FELLOW CLUB MEMBERS REMAINED BEHIND BARS AS SPRING turned to summer, and word of the Churchill Club's arrest continued to spread throughout Denmark. Despite heavy German censorship, there was no keeping the Aalborg student saboteurs out of newspapers and radio broadcasts. Whatever their age, these Churchill Club boys were organized Danish resisters, the first flesh-and-blood evidence that Danes could stand up to the German occupation. Years later a Cathedral classmate wrote, "[Their arrest] came as a bombshell to us. Today it is difficult to imagine what an enormous impact the unveiling of the Churchill Club meant to the Danish population . . . The spiritual shock effect was tremendous and lasting."

In the privacy of their homes, people talked about these boys from Aalborg. Some Danes were embarrassed that it took young students to stand up to the Nazis. Some feared that the boys had made things worse for everyone by arousing the giant. One Aalborg newspaper columnist lashed the boys for "foolish acts against foreign troops . . . They are not heroes, but fools and rascals who, through their irresponsible and unconscionable behavior, are guilty of crimes that put our city and our country in further danger . . . They should be whipped until they learn to realize this."

In contrast, many were inspired. A leaflet circulated through Aalborg's streets and shops urging citizens: "View the arrested young people and parents with sympathy! Show that you do not hate them for their actions, but rather consider them to be good Danish patriots who deserve the respect of all Danes. Create a supportive atmosphere, so the Germans will think twice about dragging them abroad or shooting them."

Kaj Munk, Denmark's most famous poet and playwright, wrote a sympathetic letter to the Pedersens' parents. The contents were published in an underground flyer that moved secretly throughout Denmark. Munk wrote: "Of course what [the boys] have done is wrong; but it is not nearly so wrong as when the government gave the country away to the invading enemy . . . Now it is time that good people in our Lord Jesus's name must do something wrong . . . I pray to God to give them cheerfulness, endurance, and constancy in the good cause."

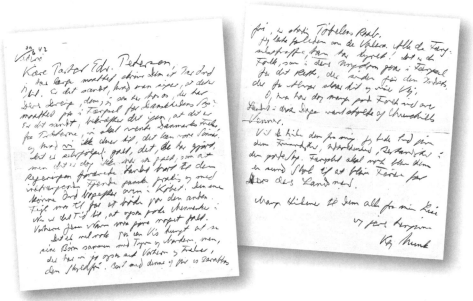

Letter from Kaj Munk to Edvard Pedersen

Kaj Munk

Kaj Harald Leininger Munk, commonly called Kaj Munk (1898–1944), was a Danish playwright, poet, Lutheran priest, and activist.

Munk's plays were mostly written in the 1920s and performed during the 1930s. He wrote about deep subjects such as religion, Marxism, and Darwin's view of evolution.

Munk at first expressed admiration for Hitler's success in getting Germans back to work during the Great Depression, but his attitude soured as he observed Hitler's persecution of German Jews.

His plays *Han Sidder ved Smeltediglen* (*He Sits by the Melting Pot*) and *Niels Ebbesen* were direct, powerful attacks on Nazism that aroused Hitler's ire. The author was arrested and subsequently assassinated by the Gestapo on January 4, 1944.

Kaj Munk is a Danish national hero. He is commemorated each year as a martyr in the Calendar of Saints of the Lutheran Church on August 14.

Kaj Munk

THE CHURCHILL CLUB BOYS GAVE TESTIMONY INDIVIDUALLY AND IN SMALL groups for a period of about ten days throughout the early summer of 1942. The presiding judge was Arthur Andersen, an experienced jurist who had been specially called to Aalborg from the Copenhagen court. He was accompanied by his secretary, a man named Silkowitz, there to produce a written record of the trial. The Churchill Clubbers remember that throughout the trial the secretary constantly interrupted the judge, asking "Is this to be written down?" or "Am I to omit this part?"

The German consul sat stiffly and in full uniform at a small writing table, carefully listening to testimony and jotting down notes. When his hand moved, eyes followed. There were no parents, journalists, or friends in the courtroom. The atmosphere was businesslike.

KNUD PEDERSEN: We had two defenders. One was Lunøes from Copenhagen. We didn't like him because he portrayed us as unruly children. Our local defender—from Aalborg—was a fat, jovial character named Knud Grunwald. He was always shouting and threatening us and warning us not to say anything against the Germans. Grunwald repeatedly came to see us in the jail, trying to prepare us for the trial. He would pace back and forth shouting, "Now you regret what you did, don't you! Answer me! Do you regret it?" He would answer himself before we had a chance to make a sound. "You sure as hell do! You better remember that the German consul in Aalborg will report straight to Berlin. Hitler will hear about this! Remember that when you are in court!"

Judge Andersen took a kinder, softer approach. One day he said to me, "Today, Knud, you're going to tell about your activities in Odense. You can tell me everything because you were only fourteen years old at the time and cannot be punished for juvenile activities." Of course I didn't mention the names of the RAF Club members, which was what he wanted.

The key to it all was the weapons; that's what they cared about. Why had we stolen them? What were we going to do with them? Our defender, and surely our government, wanted us to testify that we collected them to keep as toys or souvenirs, to show off for our friends, or just to see if we could get away with it. We were just kids looking for adventure—that's what they wanted us to say.

During one of the sessions, Judge Andersen summoned four of us to stand before him and asked us one by one why we stole the weapons. When my turn came I told the court that the weapons were not play-things to us. We planned to use them to support the British when they came to liberate us. Grunwald leaped up and asked the judge for a recess until the next day. It was granted, and court was adjourned.

That night Grunwald rushed into the jail and filled the building with his angriest speech yet. "You had almost made it!" he sputtered. "The judge could have ruled that you had no intention to use the guns! And then this idiot here—he pointed at me—testifies that your brilliant idea was to shoot the Germans *with their own guns*! You fool! Now I'm going to try to get you one more chance, and you'd better not mess up!"

The next day, Grunwald asked the judge to repeat the questions from the day before. I saw the German representative stop his hand and look up when it came my time to answer.

And of course I repeated exactly what I had said the day before.

Alf Houlberg's drawing of King Hans Gades Jail, showing the two exercise yards that were covered with netting

13

Walls and Windows

KNUD PEDERSEN: ESCAPE WAS ON OUR MINDS FROM THE VERY START. WE were not helping our country resist the German occupation by remaining in confinement. Naturally, we tested every bar and brick and lock in that old jail. Even though we were supposed to surrender our clothing to the guards each night so we wouldn't escape, we started hoarding and hiding shirts and trousers, so certain were we that somehow we'd find a way out of there.

The top of the outdoor jail yard looked like the best bet. Though the yard was enclosed by thick, high stone walls, the top was capped only by a thin wire net. If you could reach it, you could cut it. We were left un-guarded during our two daily thirty-minute outdoor sessions, so we had time to work. One morning I—the tallest—cupped my hands and boosted Uffe up onto my shoulders. He scrambled to a standing position and then, steadying himself against the wall, fumbled in his pocket for the kitchen knife we had smuggled into the yard. In a minute he had ripped a nice opening.

The idea was that one of us would pull himself out through the hole, inch along the top of the wall, and jump down into the prison commissioner's garden and scoot on out. He would make contacts on the outside and find us a place to hide. Unfortunately, the very next day one of the jailers walking across the yard glanced up and noticed the hole in the netting.

That was the end of unguarded yard time. On to Plan B.

Our ultimate goal was Sweden. The Nazis had for some reason allowed Sweden to be officially neutral. That meant that if you could get there, you were safe, at least until the Nazis changed their minds. In some parts of Denmark, near Copenhagen, you could easily see Sweden from our shore—it was a very short boat ride away. It would, however, be much harder to get there from Aalborg, where we would first have to clear the heavily guarded fjord and then proceed another six or eight hours to Swedish waters. In either case the challenge would be to find a captain who would risk going over. That would take underground contacts and probably money, of which we had neither at the moment.

Neutral Sweden

At night, while Danes and Norwegians covered their windows with black sheets and lit their streets with blue lights that couldn't be seen from the air, nearby Sweden appeared to be a carnival of light. Swedes took an officially neutral position in the war—meaning they didn't take sides. Sweden played on both teams. On the one hand, the whole German military effort depended on weapons made from millions of tons of iron ore, which Sweden exported to Germany through Norwegian harbors and the Gulf of Bothnia.

On the other hand, Sweden defied Germany by taking in war refugees, most notably the great majority of Denmark's Jews in October 1943, hours before a planned German roundup. It was logical that Sweden was the planned escape destination for the Churchill Club.

Our plan was to hide out in the legendary Thingbaek limestone cavern about twenty miles south of Aalborg. It had been purchased by a businessman who mined chalk out of a portion of it, but there were still plenty of corners to tuck ourselves away in for a few days. Our only neighbors would be the countless bats that hung from the ceilings by day and poured from the cave in chattering clouds at dusk. Like the bats, at least we would be free.

To arrange help on the outside, my sister, Gertrud, smuggled our messages to Børge's older brother, Preben. He was a classmate of Jens's at school, a well-dressed, big-talking kind of guy who repeatedly tried to convince Jens to make us stop our sabotage activities. Preben had been present at the first Churchill Club meeting, but he had never returned. He seemed horrified that his little brother had fallen in with Jens and me—as if we had corrupted poor innocent Børge. Still, he had helped us in the past and we thought we could trust him.

One visitation day we gave Gertrud a letter for Preben describing our escape plan. We asked Preben to deliver an enclosed letter Jens had written to the mine owner, seeking permission for us to stay in his mine until we could work something else out. Our final words to Preben were "Burn this letter." Preben was supposed to relay the owner's reply back to us through Gertrud. Instead he took our request straight to his parents. They were outraged. Gertrud soon brought us a letter from Preben that said, basically, "You guys are out of your minds. I'll have nothing to do with this idiocy. If you persist in this inept escape fantasy, I myself will turn you over to the police to save your lives. I'll think of something when the time is right. Sit tight."

But we didn't just "sit tight"—how could we?

EARLY ON THE MORNING OF JULY 17, 1942, KNUD AND THE OTHER BOYS WERE jolted awake by the jangling of keys, and the gruff command "Get dressed!"

KNUD PEDERSEN: They had placed our very best clothing on the stool outside the cell door. That could mean only one thing: the judge's verdict was ready. After nine weeks in the local jail, we would now learn of our future. Were we to be executed? Handed over to the Germans? Freed? Or had the Danes and Germans made some sort of deal for us to be punished in Denmark? Now we would find out.

We were ushered into vans and driven to court. Through our windows we observed trees now in full leaf, shading women in summer dresses and men in shirtsleeves. We inhaled the beautiful aroma of hot pastries sold from corner kiosks. German wagons filled with soldiers rattled toward the waterfront.

Our guards led us into the courtroom. I had no idea what our fate would be. I certainly had no regrets for what I had done—except that I had been captured. I doubt that my mates did either. We were patriots. Our enemies were the Germans who had stolen our nation and the Danes who had stood by and let them take it. Our heroes were still the Norwegians who continued to fight bravely and the outnumbered British pilots who heroically defended their country from the Nazis' relentless aerial attack. We were at war, and I was simply a soldier who had been captured. I was prepared for any outcome.

The courtroom already held the morning heat. The German monitor was at his table, face expressionless, uniform pressed, notebook open. Judge Andersen rose with a yellow paper in his hand and called us to approach his desk. Our prosecutor and our defense lawyer climbed to their feet as well. The judge read out our names and the charges against us: Wanton destruction of property. Arson. Theft of weapons from the German Army. He pronounced us all guilty as charged. We were to be punished by imprisonment at Nyborg State Prison, an adult penitentiary, southeast of Odense, nearly two hundred miles away. He did not say exactly when we would be transferred.

We each got different sentences, depending on our age and the number of counts against us. The scorecard read as follows:

Knud Pedersen: Three years, for twenty-three counts
Jens Pedersen: Three years, for eight counts (but he was eighteen
    months older than I, so he and I got the same)
Uffe Darket: Two years and six months, for six counts
Eigil Astrup-Frederiksen: Two years, for eight counts
Mogens Fjellerup: Two years, for eight counts

Helge Milo: One year and six months, for nine counts

Mogens Thomsen: One year and six months, for four counts

Our three older colleagues from Brønderslev received longer sentences, because they were adults in their twenties. The sentences were:

Knud Hornbo: Five years, for one count (passing the grenades to us)

Kaj Houlberg: Five years, for one count (same)

Alf Houlberg: Four years and six months, for four counts

We were also sentenced to pay court costs—such as the expense of employing our "brilliant" defender, Grunwald. In addition Jens, Uffe, Alf, and I were ordered to repay the German Army for all their property we'd destroyed. The tab was exactly 1,860 million kroner, or 12,538 Reichsmarks

Syv Skoleelever idømt Fængsel for Sabotage mod den tyske Værnemagt

Tre til fem Aars Fængsel, for Hærværk, Ildpaasættelse og Vaabentyverier i Aalborg

Drengene i Alderen 15—17 Aar. Ogsaa tre Voksne i Fængsel

Headlines about the Churchill Club's sentencing from an Aalborg newspaper: "Seven Schoolchildren Sentenced to Prison for Sabotage of the German Wehrmacht / Three to Five Years Imprisonment for Vandalism, Arson, and Weapons Theft in Aalborg / Boys 15–17 Years Old. Also Three Adults Imprisoned" (roughly $400,000 today). No problem, we thought. We'll have a check to you in the morning post.

According to Danish law, we would be eligible for parole after two-thirds of our sentences had been served—two years and a month in my case and Jens's. The instant that Judge Andersen banged his gavel and dismissed the case, Grunwald came up to us, waving his arms, and stuck his florid face close to ours, shouting, "Now do you regret it? *Now* do you regret it? You sure as hell do!"

As we were leaving the courtroom, Judge Andersen called my name and beckoned me back to his desk. There were tears on his eyelashes, and his voice caught as he spoke. "I learned of your attempt to escape from the jail," he said. "I have done everything I could for you. Please, promise me one thing . . . for your own good, Knud. Don't try to escape again."

FAMILY VISITATION DAY CAME JUST AFTER THE PRISONERS WERE SENTENCED. There was a big turnout—not surprising since it might be the last they would see each other for a long time. The authorities let the boys mingle as a group in the jail's front room. Kristine pastry shop sent over cream pies. Relatives brought food, smokes, and reading material. Given the circumstances, it was about as festive as a jail gets.

KNUD PEDERSEN: At one point, as prisoners and family members embraced, Alf's younger brother Tage slipped Alf a magazine. Inside was a hacksaw blade, about fourteen inches long. By the time a guard asked to see the magazine, Alf had already concealed the sharp, supple blade, dropping it into a hole in his jacket pocket that he had cut the week before when Tage told him to expect the tool. Later, waving goodbye, he walked it into his cell. We had another chance!

Jens and Alf—now cellmates—set to work that very afternoon. Forcing a slender blade back and forth against a square metal bar proved to be slow and noisy work. They could only work by daylight, for there was a strict bedtime curfew and mandatory silence at night. Alone in the cell next to them, I tried to provide as much noise as I could. I became a drummer, improvising

112

The roof of King Hans Gades Jail, showing the barred window (in foreground)
for which Jens and Alf made a dummy bar

long sessions with spoons on a metal cake box. Together we Churchill Clubbers howled every song we knew through the window bars in our cells. There were all sorts of songs about Hitler and his henchmen. One went:

> First we grab old Göring
> By his big fat calves.
> Then we knock down Goebbels—
> We don't do things by halves.
> We'll dangle Hitler from a rope
> And right beside him Ribbentrop:
> Look how stupid, all in line,
> One, two, three, four Nazi swine.

With transfer to state prison looming at some unknown date just around the corner, Jens and Alf worked like demons, sawing for our freedom. We had no way of knowing when we'd be moved—days? weeks? months? We just knew we wanted to get out of there before the bus came to take us away.

The task wasn't simply to cut out a section of the central bar in the cell window; we also wanted to *replace* the bar so that no one could notice it was missing during daylight hours. Jens ingeniously constructed the perfect mechanism—a dummy bar with a wooden pin on one end that fit into a slot in the bar. If a guard happened to pull on the bar during our weekly inspection, it would remain firm. The guard would have to push—which was unlikely—for it to move. It was a brilliant device: we could keep the bar on the window during daylight hours, and Jens and Alf could pass in and out of the jail at night. In this way we could continue with sabotage work at night and work out an escape for the entire group—without detection.

By early September we had opened up a section of the central bar big enough for a slender boy to pass through. But the color of the wooden pin was too light. It didn't match the rest of the bar. So during yard time we took a stick and smashed a window. The next day when a guard replaced the broken pane, we scraped away some of the wet caulking used to secure the pane in place, applied it to our bar, and painted it over with black ink we had in our cell. It was perfect!

And then, just after work on the bar was completed and just before we had a chance to try it out, the keys jangled again and my cell door swung open. The guard ordered me to rise and get dressed. I looked around. It was still pitch dark. What was this?

By five o'clock on that September morning, Knud and the other boys were on a bus, each of them handcuffed to a guard, motoring toward Nyborg State Prison. The authorities had spirited them away from Aalborg in the dead of night so that outraged citizens would not have time to organize a protest on their behalf. On the bus were only the six Cathedral School students and Uffe—the Houlberg brothers and Knud Hornbo had been left behind. The boys rumbled through first morning light toward a

114

bleak, faraway address with their friends and families receding behind them. It was about noon when the bus swung off the highway and they got their first glimpse of their new home.

As Churchill Club members, they had spent nearly a year striking rapidly, spinning out of harm's way, and mocking the authorities from a safe distance. One look at Nyborg State Prison told the boys that they had finally run out of cards to play.

Close-up of King Hans Gades Jail window with dummy bar

14

At Large Again?

OCTOBER 1942. DANISH POLICE AND PRISON AUTHORITIES SCRATCHED THEIR heads as they tried to make sense of the new wave of attacks on German property in Aalborg—especially cars. One German roadster was found in the fjord tipped over on its side like a beached whale. Investigators determined that somebody must have started the engine without using a key, driven it at high speed down to the harbor, and leaped out just before the auto shot out over the wharf like a missile. The German military was stirred up once again. "Get this solved at once," they harrumphed, "or else we will." It seemed as if everything was back at square one.

But who could have done such things? All the young Churchill Club boys from Cathedral School had been transferred to Nyborg State Prison. The three older prisoners—Alf and Kaj Houlberg and Knud Hornbo—were still locked in King Hans Gades Jail in Aalborg. In fact, now they were together in a single cell. Guards squinting through the peephole observed the three young men reading, chatting, piecing together model airplanes, and playing chess. They seemed to yawn and nap a lot, but jail life was hardly exciting.

The three cellmates settled down for the night like everyone else in the

Prison yard
photograph of the
Brønderslev Three:
Kaj (8), Alf (9),
Knud H. (0)

building when lights were out. Or at least that's how it looked. But as it happened, the cell they inhabited was the one with the dummy bar. When darkness and silence settled over the jail, the three became alert as cats. They got up, fished their shirts and trousers from behind the bed, and scrambled into their clothes. Each night Alf left a piece of paper on a stool in the center of the cell. On it, he scribbled his parents' telephone number and a brief message to their Danish jailers. "Please don't call the police," it read. "Call this number and we will return immediately."

Alf usually went out first. He climbed onto a chair, removed the dummy bar, squeezed through the opening, and crawled onto an awning in front of the window. Next came Knud Hornbo, who was a little pudgy. Halfway through the opening on the first attempt he got stuck. He tried not to cry out in fear or pain. Alf pulled from the outside and Kaj pushed from inside until they finally got him out, spraining his arm in the process. Kaj slid out with ease.

The rest was simple. They crawled over the wire mesh above the outdoor yard and dropped into the prison orchard. Then, after concealing themselves in dense shrubbery until they knew everything was clear, they stepped into the street as free men.

Knud Hornbo and the Houlberg brothers escaped nineteen nights in a row. The trio got so used to leaving the prison that one day they left too early and found themselves uncomfortably out on the street in broad daylight. They ducked into a movie theater and took seats. Once their eyes adjusted to the darkness, they found that they were seated among German soldiers enjoying a weekly newsreel of German battlefield heroics.

The escaped prisoners' nightly routine seldom varied. First they continued the work of the Churchill Club, smashing the instrument panels of unguarded German roadsters and setting them ablaze. When they were finished, the three walked to the Houlberg home and ate dinner with Alf and Kaj's family. The first-night shock of seeing the boys at the front door soon gave way to elation—and scheming. The boys now set to work trying to find a boat that would take them out of the Limfjorden and sail them to Sweden.

On the nineteenth night of their freedom, the young men bade the Houlbergs goodbye and started back toward the jail. As they walked they agreed it had been a lovely night: they had found and decommissioned a stylish German roadster, shorting out its electrical system. Dinner had been a festive occasion, with good food and voices raised in song. Old friends had passed in and out of their open door. They had all waved Norwegian and Danish flags. Best of all, Mr. Houlberg announced that a boat had been identified whose captain appeared to be interested in taking them to Sweden. Be ready, Mr. Houlberg had said. It could happen any day now.

And then, as they walked through the chilly morning air, a siren shattered Aalborg's predawn silence. They froze in midstep. The streets were nearly empty at 4:00 a.m., so the three young men stood out conspicuously. As the siren screamed on, their minds flooded. What should they do: Run for home? Run for jail? It was too far to reach either. They were supposed to go to a shelter during an air alert, but shelter authorities always asked for identification cards. Theirs had been confiscated at the jail. The trio ducked into the entranceway of a nearby building to gather their thoughts and make a plan. Two police officers detected their movement. One shone his flashlight into the dark recess and found six rabbit-red eyes. "May I see your identity cards?" he asked.

Soon everyone was at the police station, where stunned officers recognized but could no longer protect the three escape artists. German soldiers took them into custody and rounded up the rest of the Houlberg family. Interrogators quickly cleared up the mystery of the destroyed German property. Alf and Kaj Houlberg and Knud Hornbo were swiftly tried and convicted in German military court and transported to a German prison. Each received a sentence of more than ten years.

Danish officials loudly protested. Crimes allegedly committed by Danes on Danish soil were to be prosecuted by Danes—that was the agreement they had made. Denmark insisted that the three be returned. But German authorities weren't budging. They accused the Danish police chief of being in on the dummy window bar. Prisoners couldn't have done something like that alone, they charged. It would have made too much noise. They had to have had help.

Either way, the Churchill Club was now completely sidelined. For ten months, from marking walls with blue paint and twisting signs to stealing weapons and destroying important German assets, Denmark's first occupation resisters had bedeviled their "protectors" and awakened the courage of many Danes. But with the Brønderslev three in German captivity and the younger seven locked up at Nyborg, for now at least, it seemed the Churchill Club was history.

German soldiers outside a Danish prison, 1943

15

Nyborg State Prison

THE FORTRESS KNOWN AS NYBORG STATSFAENGSEL HELD EIGHT HUNDRED
adult men behind a maze of red-brick walls and barbed wire. Many inmates were serving sentences for violent crimes. Sometimes they were
packed four to a cell. Armed and uniformed guards patrolled a walkway
above the perimeter wall.

About noon on a September day in 1942, seven handcuffed teens
spilled out of their bus and stood uneasily while paperwork was completed.
As the bus pulled away for Aalborg, with the driver waving them good
luck, they were taken into custody by guards in black uniforms with
gold buttons. The new prisoners were ushered into the high-ceilinged
main building. One of the boys nervously cracked a joke, which brought a
guard whirling around. "All conversation is prohibited!" he shouted.

The boys were separated. Each was directed to empty the contents of
his pockets. Every possession was confiscated, even eyeglasses and family
photos. They were forced to strip naked, bend over, and receive rectal examinations.

They were issued prison uniforms—long pants and a jacket that buttoned all the way down. Knud Pedersen's arms and legs poked out as usual.

Next the barber got his turn. Clumps of the teenagers' carefully groomed hair fell to the floor beneath an electric razor. "When I lost most of my hair I also lost a big part of me," Eigil Astrup-Frederiksen later recalled.

The boys were led to the youth wing of the prison—Division K. They were the only occupants. Each boy was issued a cell number and a personal number. Knud Pedersen, now prisoner 28, stepped into cell 1. Jens Pedersen, prisoner number 30, was locked into cell 2. From then on, guards addressed the boys by their numbers—"Get up, 30!"—instead of their names.

Each cramped cell contained an iron-framed bed, a table, and a chair. The toilet was a clay pot to be cleaned by the prisoner. Each boy got two sheets of toilet paper per day. As in the King Hans Gades Jail, the cells consisted of four solid walls. The entrance was a heavy door with no handle on the inside but a peephole for looking in. A small barred window looked out onto a high red-brick wall patrolled by a Danish guard. "I would watch the guy," Knud recalled. "He was so bored that sometimes I could see him counting the number of bricks in the wall with his finger. That's all he had to do."

They were governed by countless rules, relentlessly applied. Parents could visit only once every three months, and then for only twenty minutes. Family conversations were monitored by guards. Prisoners were expected to snap to rigid attention and salute whenever the warden appeared. When it was time to go for a brief morning walk they lined up with their noses against a brick wall, arms at their sides. When released by a command, they walked ten feet apart and remained absolutely silent. A smile could cost a meal.

They were issued three skimpy meals a day. Breakfast was three slices of rye bread. Lunch was porridge. Dinner was usually a small portion of hot food. The boys quickly lost weight. "One day when I was extremely hungry I asked a guard if I could have a portion more," Eigil later wrote. "He replied angrily that we were not meant to become obese. He took away my meal. I lost twenty kilos [forty-four pounds] in the first month or two."

They followed a harsh daily routine. A clanging bell at six o'clock jarred them awake and sent them scrambling to their feet. They relieved themselves, washed their floors, and gobbled breakfast. Work started at seven. They worked ten hours a day in their cells, monotonously sorting mountains of postcards from the prison's print shop into bundles of twenty-five. They continued working until six in the evening. Every two weeks they got a hot shower. On Sundays the boys were offered the opportunity to go to church. Back home they had eagerly skipped Reverend Pedersen's church services to practice shooting the machine gun in the monastery loft, but now they jumped at any chance for a break from prison tedium. Each of the seven boys sat alone in an enclosed booth, each booth angled so that they could see the priest but not one another.

Each boy reacted to imprisonment in his own way. Eigil struggled to stave off feelings of despair. "I missed my mates," he later wrote. "The loneliness was very great. In my thoughts I convinced myself that I had done the right thing by taking part in the fight against the Germans. But in the many lonely hours came the doubt anyway, often very insidious. There was no one to talk to besides myself. The light in the cell was turned off at 9 p.m. Many times I lay in my bed and struggled with the temptation to give up, to take a razor blade and slit my wrists to stop the beating of my heart. It would not be discovered until 4 a.m., I told myself."

By contrast, Uffe Darket seemed to possess an inner cheerfulness even in the darkest of circumstances. When the others would sit on their cots despondently staring out their barred windows at the dingy snow, they could often hear Uffe singing his favorite song, which began, "There will be flowers in the window where my loved one will be living."

Knud Pedersen had no intention of taking his life, but he was far too angry to sing.

KNUD PEDERSEN: I did not adjust. I regarded the Danish jailers as German cooperators and traitors. I was in enemy land. I was punished again and again at Nyborg. Mostly they took away things. They took away my drawing materials and books from the prison library. For a month they took away "happy hour," between eight and nine at night, the one time

I could talk to my mates. Once I threw a bucket of water onto a guard's backside when he wasn't looking. He never forgave me. I smashed my own pocket watch onto the prison floor. They repaired it and sacked me five workdays. I was punished for keeping an unclean cell, for not obeying orders, for talking to my friends when ordered to shut up. And I was an easy target. I was too tall to hide behind anyone else.

They tried to strip away your identity and play with your mind. There was one little guard, pudgy and red-faced, who really hated me. He would jingle his keys outside my cell. The sound would drive me crazy, because I knew the person jingling them was free. He also had his spy hole in the door. I always had the feeling I was being watched.

One night when I was in bed I saw a mouse in my cell, illuminated by the moonbeam on the floor. It was just sitting there looking at me. I was terrified. I jumped up on the bed, screaming. Guards came running. When they realized what was going on they doubled up in laughter. I yelled back, "You can laugh only because you have guns on you. You are safe!" They slammed the door and gathered outside to watch my misery through their peephole. "That mouse is gonna get you, 28!" the chubby guard cackled. The mouse scuttled softly around the radiator pipes and seemed to try to settle in for the night. I heard every move it made. I wrapped my sheet around my head to block out the sound, but even that didn't work. The next morning Uffe came in, trapped the poor animal, and took it away.

My obsession with Grethe got worse. Now she was a goddess to me, occupying my thoughts and dreams. We were allowed to write only one letter home every two weeks, not exceeding four pages. Sometimes they were so heavily censored that almost every word was blacked out. I would use all four pages writing about Grethe. My parents wanted to know about my health; I wanted a photograph of Grethe. My sister would say that Grethe sent her greetings. I wanted her photo. Finally, my worried family was able to obtain a photo of her: there she was, seated on the ground with five puppies. It was all I ever got.

• • •

Prison drawing by Knud Pedersen of a romantic
walk with Grethe in dreams

THE BOYS HUNGERED FOR NEWS OF THE WAR—HOPING THE BRITISH WERE
gaining ground against Germany. But during family visits they were for-
bidden from discussing political events. Conversations were closely monitored by guards. The prison passed out a weekly newspaper entitled "Near
and Far Away" that presented an upbeat Nazi version of the war, along
with cheerful family stories and a page on sports. The boys read it over and
over. Parents tried to report news, but little got past the guards who monitored their conversations.

Still, information leaked in. One evening at bedtime, guards ordered the
boys to take off their shoes and hand them out the door. What was this? It
made no sense at all. The whispered explanation came during a family
visit: Knud Hornbo and the Houlberg brothers had remained in Aalborg
where they had shared the cell with the dummy escape bar that Alf and
Jens had fashioned. At night they had gone out for sabotage and had returned in the morning. But they had just been captured during one of
their escapes via the dummy window bar. Now the shoes made sense: the

warden didn't want the same thing to happen at Nyborg. Take their shoes, he had ordered his guards. Let's not give these boys any ideas.

Vi Vil Vinde (We Will Win)

In 1943, the Churchill Club's impact grew steadily outside the prison walls. The British Royal Air Force air-dropped leaflets telling the club's story all over Denmark in January and again in July. The second flyer concluded, "The schoolboys of Aalborg should be allowed to compare their actions with some of the best that take place in other occupied countries." In April the American radio series *The March of Time* dramatized the Aalborg boys' sabotage. In the radio play the tearful Danish judge ends his sentencing speech

Propaganda produced by the RAF to encourage Danish resistance fighters

with "Be brave, boys! You will never serve your whole sentence, for brighter times will soon come to Denmark and to the whole world. Be patient, you won't have to wait long."

Despite the censorship, news of the war seeped into the prison and traveled from cellmate to cellmate. Inmates heard of a major allied victory at El Alamein, in North Africa, and more progress at Stalingrad in Russia. Sometimes information came from unexpected sources.

KNUD PEDERSEN: One day in the library I met a prisoner who had been arrested a few months after us. He knew who we were and had heard that we were in Nyborg. He came pushing a book cart to each cell once every two weeks, offering books to read. A guard followed right behind him. The first time he came to me he looked into my eyes and told me to select a specific book and turn to a specific page. On that page I found a code. By spelling with combinations of underlined words and letters I was informed about the British bombing of the shipyard Burmeister and Wain in Copenhagen. This was in 1943, and we never met again after the war. He was very brave and clever to inform me as he did.

THE CHURCHILL CLUB REMAINED A POTENT SYMBOL OF RESISTANCE IN DENMARK even as its members languished behind bars. One day they were told to put on their civilian clothes and assemble in the main room. Waiting there was a formally dressed man with a familiar mild face and a head of curly hair. It was the Danish secretary of justice, Thune Jacobsen. He said he wanted to talk to them, to see how they were doing. "His tone was apologetic," Eigil recalled. "He asked us to be patient, to understand that his work was the best he could do for the benefit of all Danes. He was not a Nazi beetle, he said. The more he talked, the more he made a fool of himself. For us, he was one of the ones who aided the Germans."

The Telegram Crisis

Late in 1942, Adolf Hitler sent Denmark's king, Christian X, a warm, personal telegram congratulating the king on his seventy-second birthday. The king replied with a mere, "My utmost thanks, [signed] Christian Rex." Hitler took it as a personal slight. Enraged, the führer immediately recalled his ambassador from Copenhagen and expelled the Danish ambassador from Germany. Hitler moved Werner Best, a dedicated Nazi and Gestapo member, to Copenhagen as the high commander of Denmark.

Adolf Hitler

KNUD PEDERSEN: Thune was the worst kind of Nazi collaborator. He said our work had been useless because the British did not want Danes committing acts of sabotage against the Germans. But we knew it was a lie. The British had already organized a Danish sabotage force, and we knew it. He told us we should be grateful that we had good homes to return to, unlike most prisoners in the building. He made me sick. My letter to my parents the week after his visit was so full of spite for him that the guards returned it to me three times to rewrite it. Finally, I didn't send it at all.

One night a new batch of prisoners arrived at Nyborg. Word went from one cell window to the next. They were schoolboys from Aalborg. Their group was called Denmark's Freedom League. They had been inspired by us. Like us, they had been caught by the Danish police. They said there were many others out there, and resistance was growing. That was the best news we got, the best sign of all.

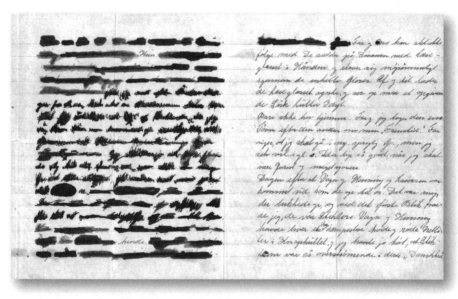

One of Knud's censored prison letters to his family with a significant portion crossed out

A PRISONER'S SENTENCE AT NYBORG WAS DIVIDED INTO THREE STAGES. STAGE 1 prisoners, the newest, had almost no privileges. Books borrowed from the prison library had to have a religious theme. Family members could write only one letter every fourteen days.

In stage 2 things relaxed a bit—inmates could go to a room to play table tennis or chess between 8 and 9 p.m. Or they could use this "happy hour," as it was called, to talk among themselves.

Stage 2 inmates could take out any book in the library. Knud Pedersen used this opportunity to catch up on classic works of literature by writers such as Goethe, Schiller, and Homer. Stage 2 prisoners also got a small garden plot that they could use as they wished. Eigil turned his into a park with castles. Jens grew a vegetable garden. Uffe made a lovely stone garden. Knud let his grow wild.

Stage 2 and stage 3 prisoners also got to have some hobby materials in the cell. Uffe at last got material to carve wooden airplanes. Knud got an artist's sketchbook. He intended on drawing set designs for theater plays, until he noticed a warning printed on the front page.

KNUD PEDERSEN: A message in bold letters read, "You are not allowed to make drawings of naked women." I filled the entire sketchbook with naked girls and when I got my porridge the next morning I used it as glue and plastered all the walls in my cells with the drawings. This was my first art exhibition. There went all my hobby materials for the next two months. I was a terrible prisoner.

ONE DAY LATE IN 1942, A TALL, SLIM, LONG-LEGGED MAN WEARING GLASSES had introduced himself to the boys as Hugo Worsaae Petersen. They could call him Mr. Worsaae. He had been sent by the prison to be their teacher since they were still of school age. They would work in a large room designated as the schoolroom. The first task would be to complete their middle school exam. Their old textbooks were en route from Aalborg, and they would study for an hour after breakfast each day, sometimes working in groups of three or four. They would study Danish, history, German, arithmetic, and geometry. They would take their written exams in their cells. Oral exams would be in the schoolroom.

After months of harshness, Mr. Worsaae was a breath of fresh air. He spoke to them as human beings. He arranged prison visits by well-known poets and convinced prison authorities to return the boys' watches, glasses, and family photos. He even got some of the guards to call them by their names rather than their numbers.

KNUD PEDERSEN: Mr. Worsaae encouraged my interest in art. He gave me many more art magazines than the regulations allowed. He read Henrik Ibsen dramas to us on Sunday afternoons. He was a wonderful actor.

He was especially kind to us at Christmastime, which meant a lot. It was the first Christmas any of us had been away from home. Memories of family and friends flooded back. I wanted to cry, but I had forgotten how. I finally discovered that by softly singing Christmas songs in my cell at night I could make the tears flow down my cheeks. I sang every song I knew and wept the whole next day.

Mr. Worsaae made sure we were treated specially on Christmas Eve, which is when we celebrated the holiday. We were summoned into the schoolroom and served a delicious pork steak and dessert. I decorated the room with a sculpture of a snow-covered hill. I drew a snow landscape on the chalkboard, too.

We gobbled so much heavy food that night that they had to feed us fried herring on Christmas day to absorb the fat. The whole day was wonderful. The day after that, while we were cleaning up, the chubby guard who was my nemesis watched me silently as I pushed my snow sculpture over to a far corner. Finally he called across the room, "Take good care of that thing, 28. . . . You're going to have to bring it back next Christmas." It was a cruel reminder that I still had more than a year to go at Nyborg. He didn't have to say that. The guards were robots.

Soon after the New Year, Mr. Worsaae saddened us boys by announcing he would be leaving Nyborg for a different assignment.

IN APRIL 1943, HELGE MILO AND MOGENS THOMSON, THE BOYS WHO HAD drawn the briefest sentences, were released from prison and taken home by their families. That left five.

Four months later, in late August 1943, inmates rushed to their windows when they heard the roar of airplanes. Eigil wrote, "I watched a large group of Allied bombers fly past! It was glorious. Now the Germans will finally get what they deserve, I thought. Three or four hours later they flew back, but not so many of them."

August 29, 1943

The sounds the Churchill Clubbers heard outside their cells on August 29, 1943, reflected an upheaval in Danish society. Throughout the spring of 1943, Germany had become increasingly frustrated with strikes by Danish workers for higher wages. When Germans cracked down with brutal countermeasures, Danes in thirty-three towns stopped working. Germans issued orders prohibiting public meetings and gatherings after dark. Danes refused to cooperate. On August 29, Germany, exasperated, took over the government of Denmark, stationing troops at railroad stations, power plants, factories, and other key places, including, as the boys discovered, Nyborg State Prison.

One day, German soldiers with rifles surged into the prison. In their cells the boys could hear the clomp of heavy boots but could not see what was going on. Rumors flew from window to window along the Division K wing: Soldiers had come to fetch them to Germany. No, they were rounding up Danish citizens who kept weapons in their homes. That actually made sense—it had long been rumored that Germans stored confiscated weapons in the Nyborg prison's giant loft.

After hours of anxious waiting, a guard came to Division K to inform them that the Danish rulers had defied orders and Germany had taken over the government. Danish authorities had refused to accept German occupation any longer. The protectorate was over. What the boys had heard from their cell windows were the sounds of Germans attacking the Danes at Nyborg Strand and Allied planes responding.

"That's how I experienced August 29, 1943," Eigil wrote. "At last our country stood up and we behaved as Norwegians did." But what would it mean to the boys in the Nyborg prison? Would they now be sent by brutal Nazi masters to German prisons? Or would their prison now be run by the Gestapo? As it turned out, the day's events changed Nyborg State Prison very little.

Danish citizens in Aalborg, August 1943, in open conflict with German occupiers

KNUD PEDERSEN: The turning point for Denmark may have been August 29, 1943, but not much at all changed for us. The main difference I saw was that the Danish guard outside my cell window—the one who paced back and forth counting bricks in the wall—was replaced by a German with a helmet, a rifle, and a battle uniform. Soon he was counting bricks just like the Dane.

THREE WEEKS LATER, ON SEPTEMBER 18, 1943, MOGENS FJELLERUP—THE Professor—and Eigil Astrup-Frederiksen were released. Months later, Uffe Darket, too, said his goodbyes and the Churchill Club at Nyborg was down to the Pedersen brothers. They were transferred to a different unit, nearer the adult prisoners.

The Rescue of Danish Jews

On September 28, 1943, a German diplomat secretly informed Danish resistance leaders of Nazi plans to deport the Danish Jews to German concentration camps for mass execution. Danes quickly organized a nationwide effort to smuggle Jews by sea to neutral Sweden. Tipped off to the German plans, most of Denmark's Jews left Danish cities by train, by car, or on foot. Non-Jewish Danes hid them in homes, hospitals, and churches until they could be moved to Sweden. Within a two-week period, fishermen helped ferry some 7,200 Danish Jews and 680 of their non-Jewish family members to safety in Sweden.

The only Churchill Club member directly affected was Eigil. His mother was Jewish, and the family was deeply concerned. A mere ten days after Eigil was released from Nyborg, he remembered, "Our parish priest advised us to go underground . . . We left home and stayed with friends. Fortunately, the Germans didn't catch us, so after some days we moved back home again."

A reenactment of the October 1943 boatlift of Danish Jews to Sweden, from a Swedish film produced in 1945

In America, an exaggerated version of the Churchill Club's story appeared in the September 1943 issue of *True Comics* under the title "The Boy Saboteurs" (see also page 180)

16

First Hours of Freedom

ON MAY 27, 1944, KNUD AND JENS PEDERSEN WERE RELEASED FROM NYBORG State Prison. On one of the very last days before he was released, Jens took his written student examination for university admission from his cell. Guards explained to adult inmates that number 30 was attempting something extremely difficult, something that required great concentration. As a gesture of respect, the whole section of the prison remained silent during the morning hours as Jens worked. Even the guards refrained from jingling their keys.

He got the highest possible score. A Nazi-controlled newspaper complained in print that Jens Pedersen should not have had the opportunity to take the test. His chance, said the writer, proved that it was now possible for a saboteur to be a judge in Denmark.

Knud and Jens had each served two years and a month. Though they were no longer prisoners 28 and 30, there were huge adjustments ahead for both of them.

KNUD PEDERSEN: It is difficult to imagine or to describe how long the last days of prison were. The minutes crawled by. Each hour took twice as long as the one before. Finally, the moment came when our names were called, the doors to our cells were pulled open, and we were escorted to the gate where our parents stood to receive us. I think they were shocked by our appearance. My street clothing hung like drapery over my thin frame. My hair was barely long enough to put a comb through. Mother could not hold the tears back.

We walked through the city of Nyborg to the railway station and caught a train to Odense. There, Knud Hedelund—"Little Knud"—our partner in the RAF Club way back at the beginning of our resistance, was waiting with his parents to greet us warmly. They drove us by car—a rare treat in wartime—to a tremendous party in our honor. There were Danish flags on the table and roast duckling on the plates. Best of all were ripe home-grown garden tomatoes, specimens so rich and abundant that Jens and I—after two years of bread and porridge—spent much of our first free night rushing back and forth to a toilet.

After toasts in our honor we stepped outside and took a walk in the moonlight with Little Knud. At last here was our chance to find out what had happened to our brothers in the RAF Club. Where was our cousin Hans Jøergen? And Harald Holm? Had they continued to attack the German war machine? Was everyone still alive? Were they free or had they been captured?

It had been nearly two years since we had heard from the RAF Club. My cousin Hans Jøergen, who like me was eighteen years of age now, had written to us all the way through our jail stint in Aalborg, exchanging coded war bulletins with Jens. But then we lost contact with him at Nyborg. For some reason he quit writing altogether. His final message had said simply, "We continue."

The three of us walked back among the Hedelund family's tomato greenhouses, and Little Knud unloaded what he knew.

The RAF Club had expanded while we were in prison, taking on more classmates from the Odense school. They made many strikes, the most powerful of which happened in Naesby, on the outskirts of Odense. There, the Germans had taken over an auto plant and retooled it to make mobile homes for their soldiers on the eastern front. The factory was an obvious target for the RAF Club. They chose the night of the Hans Christian Andersen Nightingale Festival to attack, on an evening when Odense's entire populace was absorbed in celebrating Denmark's most famous author.

Several RAF Club boys, one of them Hans Jøergen, entered the factory from the rooftop and discovered inside a treasure of combustible materials—paint thinner, paint itself, and best of all gas bottles! What a gift they could make for the Third Reich! They piled up some rags, soaked them with gas, and climbed a ladder they had placed inside back up onto the roof.

From the roof, they tossed a match or a lighted rag; then they dropped to the ground and took off running. In a matter of moments, a mighty explosion shook the building.

The other party guests were calling for us to go back inside, but this was too important. We would have to travel to Aalborg the next day, and here was our only chance to find out. We ignored the calls and stayed outside to hear more.

KNUD HEDELUND TOLD THE PEDERSENS THAT WHEN MEMBERS OF THE RAF Club turned eighteen, some wanted to go to England and enlist with British forces. But it wasn't easy. They would have to flee Denmark to Sweden, and then make an underground arrangement to continue to Britain.

Though they didn't know it, their fate had already been sealed. One of the RAF Club's younger members, naively believing that Danish authorities would help them escape to Sweden, had sent an anonymous letter to Danish police that read: "Orla Mortensen [the name of one of the RAF members] is involved in major sabotage." And he gave Orla's full name and address.

Within hours Orla was in custody and others were on the run. One RAF Club member leaped out a window when police rang his doorbell. The boy who'd written the letter was tracked down on his bicycle. Hans Jøergen was overtaken by a Danish policeman after a foot chase across a field.

They were immediately convicted by a German court martial. A month later the RAF Club boys sat in prison glumly awaiting their fate and shooting suspicious glances at each other—who had been the rat? Soon these RAF Club members, including Hans Jøergen, were transported to the German-run Western Prison in Copenhagen, in a special wing reserved for political prisoners, those convicted of having committed acts of resistance.

As they started back toward the party, Knud Hedelund confessed that he was deeply worried about Hans Jøergen and the others. It was well-known that at Western Prison serious resisters were shipped to a special place—later called the Memory Park—where they were roped to trees and shot to death. With that in mind, they stepped back inside.

A drawing by Hans Jøergen
Andersen of his cell in Odense

KNUD PEDERSEN: We sat back down at the table to listen to more speeches and accept more tributes to our courage. But Little Knud's report had pulled us back into a reality that, closeted as prisoners, we had not faced in a long time. We were still occupied by an enemy, and we were still at war.

After the final speech and the last toast, I was shown by my hosts to my bedroom. I closed the door and lay down on my bed, head pounding.

For the first time in years I was lying in a room whose windows had no bars. It was like a new life. Perhaps the adults who kindly gathered around us that evening to celebrate our release from prison wanted to give us the impression that there was peace in the world, so that for a short while at least, we could taste freedom. But in the minutes before I fell asleep I could only think about my brothers. Where was Hans Jøergen tonight? Where was Alf? Were they alive? I fell asleep freshly reminded that we were still on the road to an uncertain future and that there was still so much work to do.

At secret locations, British planes dropped weapons containers for Danish partisans

17

Better on the Inside

THE NEXT AFTERNOON KNUD AND JENS PEDERSEN HOPPED DOWN FROM THE
Odense passenger car, took the family luggage off the train, and helped
their parents step onto the pavement. As the train pulled away the quartet
began to walk through the cavernous station, finally pushing through the
arched doorway and out into the sunlit streets of Aalborg.

It was May 1944. Familiar streets told of a Denmark that had changed
radically while the brothers were behind bars. Shop owners who had sold
goods to German soldiers in the old days now stared through the windows
of empty stores. Others stood out front and swept the sidewalks, looking left and right for a German customer. They were stigmatized as traitors now.

Exactly two years earlier, when the Churchill Club members had been
arrested, the boys were among the very few who had stood up to the German oppressors. They had been caught, but not before they had set the
ball in motion. Now a resistance was in full swing.

There were eight times as many acts of sabotage in 1943 as there had
been in 1942. By 1944, so many acts of violence had been committed

against German property that Germany had declared Denmark "enemy territory."

Aalborg had become a hotbed of resistance. Residential gardens bulged with buried guns, smuggled from abroad, tooled at home, or stolen from the Germans. Underground newspapers, at last telling the truth about the war, flew from small, mobile, concealed presses. Massive labor strikes challenged German authority.

Night after night British planes parachuted tubes of weapons at prearranged spots throughout Denmark. Back in 1942, when the Churchill Club members were captured and jailed, shocking the nation, Germany had seemed invincible. Now, two years later, with Norwegian conditions achieved at last, Goliath was teetering.

The Pedersens walked on to the monastery. They dropped their bags and banged on the front door. A voice rang out, received an answer, and the door opened a crack. Then it flew all the way open and there were open arms and broad smiles of welcome for Knud and Jens.

The boys soon discovered that no place in Aalborg had changed more than their own home. Never a restful place, the monastery had become a full-blown resistance cell. Couriers were constantly depositing or picking up coded messages. Saboteurs hid inside the monastery, using it as a safe house.

Edvard Pedersen proudly conducted his sons through the new emergency escape route, out through the back door, up the stairs to the loft—where a fully loaded rifle rested at the ready—and on to the coil of rope at the rear of the chapel building that could be used to drop down onto a back street.

Knud soon realized his family had changed, too.

KNUD PEDERSEN: My mother had become the master of the house. It was she who opened the door when the knock sounded and you didn't know who was on the other side. Father allowed the monastery to become a safe house for resisters, but every week he put us all in danger. He damned the bloody Germans in his Sunday sermons, almost taunting them. The

144

Sunday after a failed attempt on Hitler's life, Father observed from the pulpit, "Well, the devil looks after his own, doesn't he?" His parishioners warned him to back off. They said a full church on Sunday was a perfect site for a "clearing murder," the revenge mass execution the Germans typically carried out when a single Nazi informer was shot by the resistance.

Father ignored them. He brandished the big Colt revolver given to him by the resistance to protect himself. He showed it off to friends who came to the monastery. Once when he was messing around it went off, sending a bullet tearing into our bookshelves. It lodged in volume three of the five-volume *History of the Danish People*. That bullet passed only a few centimeters from Mother's head.

Action sizzled throughout Denmark. On June 6, just two weeks after Knud and Jens were released from Nyborg, resistance fighters bombed the Globus factory on the outskirts of Copenhagen, halting production of the V-2 rockets that had been hammering London.

Days later, saboteurs from the Danish resistance group Borgerlige Partisaner (BOPA) blew up the Riffel Syndicate factory, makers of machine guns for the Germans.

Jens had his mind fixed on college, but Knud wanted to jump back into the thick of the resistance. His parents worried. To them, Knud needed rest, not action. The family scraped up enough money to rent a summer house in a small seaside village. Long summer days and evenings with family, walks in the sunshine—that's what the boys needed to heal, they thought.

KNUD PEDERSEN: I was totally lost at first. I didn't know what to do. I was as lonely as ever for a soul mate, maybe even more so because just after I got back I met Grethe again and I instantly realized I wasn't in love anymore. She was riding down the street on her bicycle and stopped to greet me. I had spent more than two years totally obsessed with this person and now, strangely, all the feelings had vanished. Where did that leave me?

That was what I was puzzling over when, in the seaside town of Hurup,

I met a young girl vacationing alone with her father. The old man was sitting on his porch in an armchair with a glass of whiskey, singing. Next to him was his daughter, Patricia Bibby, seventeen, dark haired, and beautiful.

We started talking. It turned out she lived in Aalborg and went to Cathedral School. They were British and had been trapped in Denmark by the German invasion. After a day or two I went back and invited her to the beach. We spent the whole day walking among the dunes and sunbathing and talking. We lay side by side, and at times there was less than an inch between our fingertips. I couldn't work up the nerve to span that inch for fear of ruining the whole thing.

But we talked. That is, I talked and she listened. She was the greatest listener. I could tell her anything, about prison, about my actions against the Germans, about my dreams. She laughed with a great laugh and encouraged me to hold nothing back. She made me feel like a soldier, even though I had spent much of the war behind bars, too young to enlist and with no army to enlist in anyway. I would have told her anything.

PATRICIA BIBBY HAD WANTED TO MEET KNUD PEDERSEN. "EVERYONE AT school knew who he was. I admired the stance he took, and he was very good-looking. I made a point to get to know his sister, Gertrud. I invited her to my house, and found out that the Pedersens were going to Hurup for the summer. I maneuvered my father to going there instead of where we were planning to go. It's true that Knud and I met by chance, but I was there on purpose. I loved listening to him and being with him. I found him exciting. Alive and fun. Did I feel anything for him? Oh, yes, I did. He was tall and slender and funny, and he had an idea every two minutes. When we were lying on the beach he said, 'I don't know why we can't have suitcases with four little wheels.' Then it was 'Why can't we get toothpaste to pop out of a bottle?'"

According to Patricia, Knud also talked about his resistance experiences, about his obsession with a girl while he was in prison, about taking the guns from the German soldiers and going out at night to do sabotage. "I was

Patricia Bibby at Cathedral School graduation, 1946

not mature enough at seventeen to sense that he was in trouble, that prison had left him deeply shaken. He talked about jail through amusing stories, like the one about the guard who told him to polish his latrine until it shone 'like your mother's best vase.' I laughed, but I couldn't feel his pain. Not yet."

KNUD PEDERSEN: After the summer holidays Pat became a daily guest in the afternoon in the monastery, visiting Gertrud. I did my best to win her heart. We visited in my room a lot. I showed her my paintings and produced a couple of romantic paintings especially for her.

One night in the winter between 1944 and '45, Patricia's father died, leaving her alone in the world. My mother immediately invited her to move into the monastery, which she did.

Living with us changed the whole chemistry. Now she became a sort of half-sister to me, though I was still in love with her. Jens came home from university in Copenhagen, and of course he fell instantly in love with Pat. That was a given: anything I wanted, Jens would try to get. One night Pat came and showed me a gift she had gotten from Jens—a ring inset with a big green stone. I was unable to speak. My only hope was that she was not in love with him, but I was not going to ask. That would break our code: the way we were, if she had something to tell me, Pat would do so.

ONE WINTER NIGHT ABOUT TEN O'CLOCK, THE FAMILY HEARD A BANGING AT THE monastery's front door. Mrs. Pedersen nervously cracked it open upon a snow-covered young man on skis. He was panting hard, sending plumes of vapor into the cold air. He introduced himself as Karl August Algreen Moeller, a polytechnical student from Copenhagen University. He had just skied thirty-five miles from the village of Randers, pursued by the Gestapo. He had been given the monastery's address as a safe house. Please, he asked. Could they shelter him?

He was heartily welcomed and installed in an extra bed in Knud's room.

The SOE

The Special Operations Executive (SOE), a British covert group, worked with all European resistance movements. Danish resistance activists received British training to carry out sabotage acts. The SOE was extremely disciplined, with a very firm command structure. The British insisted on control. British Royal Air Force planes dropped thousands of containers of weapons onto Danish soil in 1944 and 1945. Danes who were caught collecting weapons were shot on the spot or sent to German concentration camps. When the Churchill Club members were arrested in 1942, many Danish police were trusted German collaborators. But by the time the Pedersens were released in 1944, many Danish police refused German orders and were helping the resistance. It was another sign of how greatly things had changed while the boys were locked up.

A container with weapons dropped by the British SOE over Denmark to support the resistance, 1945

KNUD PEDERSEN: Karl was the resistance saboteur I longed to be. His work began each evening in my father's office when the news service from BBC to Denmark came on the radio. Karl telegraphed radio messages to the British group Special Operations Executive (SOE) every day from different addresses in Aalborg—though, curiously, never from the monastery. The British commanders sent coded messages through the radio broadcasts, like "Your grandmother wants a cup of tea" or "There is no more air in the front wheel on your bike." Each message

Karl August Algreen Moeller

signaled the movement of resistance forces. "Your grandmother wants a cup of tea" could mean "Be at a certain farmer's field at 9:00 p.m., when RAF airplanes will drop weapons containers."

These communications and the weapons deliveries they enabled were the very lifeblood of Denmark's resistance to the Nazis. Karl had to send his messages at very high speeds because the Gestapo went around with tracking antennas on their shoulders trying to locate where these messages were being transmitted from. Karl was well-known and hotly pursued by the Gestapo.

Karl and I became friends, but we could not be confidants. He never said where he was going when he left the house each afternoon, and I never asked. I knew that each day before he left he was visited by a superior—a guy in a trench coat—who handed him the script for his coded radio message to London that day.

At night Karl and I lay in our beds talking. I hungered to be part of the organized resistance, and I would tell him all my sabotage ideas. One night we discussed the possibilities of throwing a bomb from a railway bridge. I told him the Germans always had Danish prisoners in the first train car, so we'd have to wait until at least the third passed under us. He just smiled.

All conversation froze whenever we heard a car approaching our windows. The monastery was on a street corner, so every car had to gear down to make the turn. The headlights would sweep around the corner, and the driver would shift. Is it slowing down? Did it stop? Lying there listening to those cars with Karl, I was terrified for the first time. The old Churchill Club actions did not frighten me, but maybe prison had changed me. Every time I heard a smooth-purring private car operating with high-quality gas, I told myself, "That could only be one of two things: the Gestapo or a doctor." Our ears were attuned to the slightest sound. If the engine stopped totally, we'd have to run for it. So we would lift our heads just a little whenever the headlights passed to try to get a peek. It was so frightening.

Weapons Drops

In early 1943, a liaison office in Stockholm, Sweden, was set up to link the Danish Resistance and the SOE. The idea was to coordinate the dropping of weapons into Denmark. The first receivers were peasants from Jutland, the very northern part of Denmark. Plans were made through coded radio broadcasts. On target nights, peasants waited on dark, lonely heaths until they heard the drone of an aircraft. They signaled the low-flying planes in with electric torches and ran to gather up the objects that floated down to them on twenty-foot parachutes. Then they spirited the canisters filled with weapons away, hopefully before German soldiers—who could also hear the planes—had time to react.

One night Karl didn't return to the room. He never came back. A few months later, just after Liberation Day, I learned that he had been chased up a staircase into a loft and surrounded by Gestapo officers. He shot and killed two of them and then put the gun to his own head.

After liberation his body was found in a grave at the military airport. There was a note to his parents. I was called out to identify him, and it was an awful sight. He had been bound with wires around his legs and arms. We brought him to the chapel. A few days later I was in the car following him to the small village where he'd been born. There were flowers all along the street to his family home and all the Danish flags were at half-mast.

Karl August Algreen Moeller's Farewell Letter

Dear Mother and Father,

I am going to die now and I am quite afraid; but I believe that God will give me strength to die as a Christian and a Dane in the battle for Denmark.

I pray that He will bless you. I believe I did my utmost and would rather die than be captured. They are outside now and I will confront them.

I commit my soul to God.

Karl

I later learned that when Karl found out that the whole Pedersen family was working underground he asked his commander to be moved from the monastery. He did that to spare us.

THE CHURCHILL CLUB BOYS NO LONGER GOT TOGETHER AFTER THEIR RELEASE. Each made his own adjustment. In 1943, Helge Milo and Eigil Astrup-Frederiksen enrolled in eleventh grade at Cathedral School and tried to get on with their studies. The faculty was divided as to whether to let them back into school. A classmate remembers that on Helge's first day in English class, the teacher, a known Nazi sympathizer, addressed the new boy with lofty authority in his voice.

"I think I see a new face among us . . . Who are you?"

"My name is Helge Milo."

"And where are you coming from?"

"Nyborg . . . Nyborg State Prison."

The teacher launched into a rant as if no one else was in the room. Among the things students heard him fuming about were "misguided youth."

Mogens Fjellerup—the Professor—also went back to Cathedral School. Before he was admitted, he was required to swear that he would do nothing to harm the school. "Perhaps it was wrong," he later wrote, but he did swear. There was no reason for a Churchill Club anymore, now that the resistance was professional and effective. "There was no longer any chance for adventuresome groups [of teenagers]," Mogens wrote. But he missed the excitement. "So went the time," he said, "and it was just as slowly as in prison."

Eigil got off to a smooth start in Aalborg. He was greatly relieved that his family had escaped the Nazis during their attempt to round up Denmark's Jews. Better still, his girlfriend, Birthe, had waited for him. At first, Cathedral School provided a welcome if unexciting routine.

And then one day a friend asked him if he would be interested in resistance work. Eigil found himself accepting. He was taken into a unit, trained to handle weapons, and assigned to deliver sensitive messages from place to place.

After several successful deliveries he was asked to deliver documents to Sweden, traveling on a boat with an old man and another boy about his age. The night before departure the documents were delivered to his grandfather's house. Early the next morning the Gestapo boots came thundering up the stairs. Fists hammered on the door, and shouts ordered them to open. Eigil stuffed the documents in his shoe and climbed through the third-floor window and out onto the roof with Gestapo officers close behind. Soon cornered, Eigil said a prayer and attempted to leap down onto a garden shed. He missed, shattered his leg on the pavement, and soon found himself a captive once again, this time in a German-run hospital.

After the summer break in 1944, Knud also reenrolled at Cathedral School, but his heart was not into studying. Having been imprisoned the longest, Knud was a grade behind the other Churchill Clubbers.

"He never bothered to take any books to school," Patricia Bibby recalled later. "He was an artist, a painter. Here was a young man who had translated Milton's *Paradise Lost* into Danish while he was in prison. He was too old to go back to high school."

Knud's social network had collapsed. Jens was studying in Copenhagen. Alf and Kaj Houlberg and Knud Hornbo were still in prison, though at least Alf and Kaj had been returned to Danish cells after six months in Germany. Hans Jøergen was a Nazi captive, surely suffering—if he was even still alive.

Knud hungered to join the SOE-led organized resistance but couldn't find a way in. He was well-known throughout Aalborg as a Churchill Club leader, but resistance professionals saw him as a security risk.

These were different days. The new resistance movement was built on discipline. Could Knud Pedersen take orders? Could he hold his temper? Could he function within a command structure?

Knud tried one door after another. All were closed. His spirits plunged; his confidence bottomed.

"A couple of times his mother called me," Patricia Bibby recalls. "He had locked himself inside his bedroom door and would not come out. 'Would you please see if you can help?' she asked. I stood outside the door talking, trying to get him to open it. He had torn his paintings and writings. He said they were no good. That they were worthless. That he felt worthless. It was a terrible depression he had. And we would talk."

One afternoon Knud went outside for a walk and drifted into a crowd that had formed outside the Gestapo headquarters downtown. As he watched from the fringes his eyes were drawn to the sewer manhole cover in the street outside the building. An idea came to him.

KNUD PEDERSEN: I remembered that in the movie *Oliver Twist*, London's sewers were broad tunnels through which people traveled. I thought surely the tunnels of Aalborg passed under the Gestapo headquarters. I was still thinking about this a bit later when I passed a toy store and stopped to look at the scene in the window, an electric railroad. I got an idea: I bet a toy train with a tender and three or four wagons loaded with PE2 dynamite on rails leading beneath the Gestapo building might work.

That's how desperate I was to be a part of the organized resistance. Of course, the rational side of me knew this was a harebrained idea, a hopeless enterprise. But ever since I had come home from the jail I had tried without success to introduce myself to the organized resistance movement built up by the SOE. The answer was always the same: I was supposed to be a "security risk."

From the toy store I walked to Aalborg's city office building. I found the municipality's technical division and asked the clerk if they had a blueprint of the sewer system in Østeråstreet.

"For what use?" he asked.

"Well, I would just like to study the size of the tubes."

"Oh, you think it is like Paris where you can walk around, right?"

By this time all the young engineers in the office were gathering around and laughing, but through an open door I could glimpse the senior engineer in his separate office behind the clerk's counter. He wasn't laughing at all.

Turned out he was the chief of the SOE's Kings Company (K Company) in Aalborg. He knew all about me. After I left, he turned to one of his colleagues who was also a member of this K Company and said, "It would be better to have Mr. Pedersen on the inside than the outside."

The next day a man came to offer me a command in the resistance. I became the leader of K Company, Division B, Group Number 4. Our job was to move ammunition, weapons, and explosives from hiding place to hiding place to avoid German detection. At last I received weapons training, which included taking apart and reassembling machine guns. I learned to use American-made grenades, too, which looked like pineapples. I could now operate the things we had stolen with the Churchill Club.

Gertrud Pedersen, Patricia Bibby, and Inger Vad Hansen: Resistance Fund-raisers

Patricia Bibby became an effective fund-raiser for the resistance, as did Knud's sister, Gertrud, and their friend Inger Vad Hansen. The three girls jumped at Knud's proposal that they raise funds to support the underground newspapers that were countering German propaganda. Together they visited wealthy Aalborg citizens—usually businessmen—and engaged them in conversations that ended in a pitch for funds. The risk was that they never knew for sure the private sympathies of the people they were talking to. When they, or their superiors in the resistance, sensed danger, the girls were ordered to go underground.

"We would stay with friends," Patricia recalls. "During such times I would meet my father in the churchyard once a week so he would know I was still alive. We would pass without looking and never spoke."

Wealthy donors wondered how they could be assured their money would actually go to the official resistance. The girls offered them a code name, promising that the name would appear on a certain page in the underground paper *Frit Danmark*. It was a secret receipt. Inger kept the list in her head, never writing it down, and memorized in code.

The three girls collected many thousands of Danish kroner for the underground movement.

Our first assignment was to move a weapons cache from a church at the other end of Aalborg into the monastery's chapel. It was dangerous work, for the Germans had taken over a school just across the street from the church that housed the weapons. At all hours young soldiers sat in the windows, smoking, laughing, and peering down on everything that went on—including our repeated bicycle journeys from the church, during which we carried bulky objects wrapped in black paper.

One afternoon just a few days after my unit was formed, I got word that a member of our group had probably been captured by the Gestapo. They would try to torture information out of him. We had to move the weapons at once. We started wrenching up the floorboards and pulling the weapons out. We were wrapping them in black paper for transport when there was a great hammering at the door! Guns and grenades lay scattered all over the church. The banging continued. One of our people unwrapped a machine gun and took a position with his back against the altar. Another grabbed a weapon and crawled behind the pulpit.

Heart hammering, I opened the door. There stood a member of the church choir. It was time for practice, he said. He took a look into the church and knew in a flash what was going on. He offered to help us, and we told him he could help most by spreading the word that practice had been canceled. By late afternoon we had moved it all—including rifles for thirty-five men—to the monastery chapel.

On the evening of May 4, 1945, I was out on the street when I heard a radio blaring through an open window. The announcer said that the Germans had surrendered and that our liberation would take place the following morning. I saw people turning their lights on and off and cheering through their windows and dancing and thronging out of their buildings into the street. Soon our platoon received orders to gather at the monastery. All thirty-five unit members showed up. We were ordered to sit tight at the monastery for now. Early the next morning we would take possession of the Aalborg airport—the Germans' great prize.

That night we carried all the weapons from the chapel down into the drawing room. The strong smell of oil from bazookas and rifles wafted through parlors and sitting rooms. When we were done, Mother served coffee and Father distributed hymnals. I ended the war at the monastery chapel just a few meters away from the room in which the Churchill Club was born—singing hymns with the men of my K Company group. I was eighteen.

Liberation!

At 8:30 p.m. on May 4, 1945, Danish announcer Johannes G. Sørensen paused in his BBC nightly news broadcast to read a telegram he had just been handed. It was but two sentences long:

FIELD MARSHAL MONTGOMERY ANNOUNCES THAT ALL GERMAN FORCES IN NORTHWEST GERMANY, HOLLAND, AND DENMARK HAVE SURRENDERED. THE SURRENDER BECOMES EFFECTIVE AT 8 O'CLOCK TOMORROW MORNING.

Five years of occupation by the Germans were over. Danes everywhere took to the streets, laughing and crying, dancing and singing. People stripped the blackout curtains from their windows, burned them in the street, and replaced them with candles of joy.

Danes shredding and burning the flag of their occupiers

Liberation Day, May 5, 1945

18

Our Evening with Mr. Churchill

AFTER LIBERATION CAME THE TASK OF TRANSITIONING DENMARK FROM AN occupied nation to a free country. Some German soldiers refused to surrender. Danish Nazis, despised by their countrymen and with nowhere to go, had no choice but to fight to the bitter end. In the weeks after liberation, thousands of German soldiers just hung around Denmark, sometimes still running things, reluctant to return to a Germany that remained at war in many parts of the globe and whose cities, pounded by Allied bombers, had been reduced to smoldering ruins.

In the end, most Germans marched out of Denmark, laying down their weapons at the border. In the weeks following liberation, 15,000 accused collaborators were arrested and tried in Danish courts. Of these, 13,521 were found guilty and 46 were executed.

The organized resistance helped manage the swing back to a Danish-run government. As a company group leader, Knud Pedersen was ordered to take his men to a building at Aalborg's civilian airport to oversee the transition from German to Danish management. He expected the change to be well under way, but when he and his men arrived, they were shocked to find that the airport was still run by Germans.

Danish citizens were still flashing identity cards to German masters just as they had throughout occupation. Knud and his men moved rapidly to take over.

KNUD PEDERSEN: I gave the order to confiscate all identification cards and give Germans employed there two hours to gather their belongings and depart. The German commander came out boiling mad, and I told him to leave at once. Within minutes a crowd of motor traffic was closing in on us from all over the airport—English jeeps with British Tommy soldiers and Danish resistance cars spilling over with officers.

My chief canceled my orders at the airport base and ordered that everyone's ID cards be given back. I was ordered into a car and driven to our headquarters, where I was lectured.

I had exceeded my authority, my chief said. I had strayed outside of command. "You will obey orders from this moment on," he said.

German troops departing Denmark

A possible Nazi collaborator under arrest by Danish police

I refused.

How could I obey? The scene at the airport was firsthand evidence that elements of the resistance had been corrupted. Now reports were coming in that Danish authorities had already freed German sympathizers from some prisons. Was that what we had fought for?

I found other group leaders who were just as frustrated as I was. Together we wrote out a list of five demands to govern the transition:

1. All Germans should be put behind bars.
2. Danes should stop trading with Germans.
3. Collaborators should be arrested at once.
4. Food for German soldiers should be rationed.
5. The resistance should be cleansed of corruption.

I took the five points to a printer, who promptly left the room and called the police. My company chief found me, relieved me of my command, and confiscated my weapons and ammunition. Now I was on the street again, with no command and no future in the resistance. I glumly returned to the monastery and mulled my options. None looked good.

I was still in a dark cloud a few afternoons later when, to my total surprise, a car from K Company came screeching up to the monastery. The same men who had dismissed me days before now hailed me warmly and returned my machine gun, ammunition, and signs of grade. What could have happened?

It turned out that Major General Richard Dewing, the British commander of all military forces in Denmark, had come to my rescue—not that he meant to. Now that liberation had come, he wanted to meet the legendary Churchill Club, Denmark's first resisters. He would soon be visiting Aalborg. He ordered his staff to round up as many Clubbers as they could find and have them at the Hotel Phoenix at a certain time.

We were all astonished by the meeting. Uffe Darket told us that a British Royal Air Force plane had shown up at his post in Germany, with a pilot whose orders were to take him to Aalborg, Denmark. There was no explanation, just "Let's go." Helge, Uffe, the Professor, Alf, all of us— everyone had a similar story.

General Dewing meeting with the Churchill Club (the general is at the head of the table, Knud is to his immediate right)

On the day of the meeting we were seated at a long table in the hotel dining room with General Dewing at the head. He greeted us individually, by name. He said he wanted to know our whole story, from Odense to Aalborg to Nyborg State Prison and beyond. So we detailed our lives first as angry schoolboys, then as increasingly bold saboteurs, and then as prison inmates. We gave him the late-night raid on the Fuchs Construction Company's headquarters at the airport, and remembered how good it felt to use the framed photo of Hitler as a trampoline. We told stories of stolen weapons, ruined autos, and scorched railway cars. He laughed out loud when we came to the dummy bar on the cell window at King Hans Gades Jail. He asked question after question. Finally, he pushed his seat back and stood. "This is a good story," he said, saluting us. "I'll tell it to Mr. Churchill."

WINSTON CHURCHILL DID INDEED HEAR THE STORY, BUT PROBABLY NOT FROM General Dewing. Five years later, in the autumn of 1950, Denmark was no longer preoccupied with the war. For the first two or three years after liberation, the air had been thick with accusations and demands for justice to the traitorous collaborators, but now there was a sense in the population of getting on with things, that the horrible hour was at last behind them, that the sun was shining again. The Churchill Club had scattered, and there had never been a reunion. Most of its members were launching careers and starting families.

KNUD PEDERSEN: I had moved to Copenhagen. At that time I was taking a few classes at law school, but my real love, as always, was art. I spent all the time I could painting and talking late into the night, debating and learning about new trends in modern art. Like all young students in Copenhagen at that time, and especially art students, I barely had enough money to buy a cup of coffee. To get by, I got up each morning at five to deliver newspapers, and I also worked in a brewery, sorting empty bottles. It was about as challenging as the work I had done at Nyborg State Prison.

One night I got out of a class and was hurrying across a city square to meet some friends when I glanced up at the electronic headline wrapped around the top of a newspaper building. It read, "Churchill Club to Meet Winston Churchill."

I stopped. Pedestrians rushed past me as if I were a stone in a stream. I stumbled to a telephone box in the middle of the square, but I couldn't scrape up the right coins to call home. Just then, my glance went to a broad white banner stretched across the front of a hotel next to the newspaper building: CHURCHILL CLUB MEETING HEADQUARTERS. I gave my name to the lady at the reservation desk and asked for a telephone. She said they had been trying to find me all day.

Old clubmates trickled in through the night and the next morning. Unfortunately, Jens was working as an engineer in India and could not attend. Some were university students and still knew each other, but I had lost touch with nearly everyone. Several were fathers now—I hoped that was in my future.

SIR WINSTON CHURCHILL'S MAIN BUSINESS IN COPENHAGEN WAS TO ACCEPT AN award for outstanding contributions to European culture. The award ceremony would be held the following night at Copenhagen's three-thousand-seat KB Hall. The Churchill Club members were still puzzled as to exactly how all this had come about, but they went along with the attention and the opportunity to meet Churchill. The event's sponsor was a newspaper whose reporters and photographers had endless ideas for publicizing the event, including giving them all big Winston Churchill cigars to smoke while camera shutters snapped.

The following day, while Winston Churchill and his family lunched with the Danish king at the castle, the Churchill Club enjoyed a luncheon in their honor at the hotel. The master of ceremonies was Ebbe Munck, a resistance hero who had been the contact between the secret British sabotage organization SOE and the Danish military intelligence. When he spoke, the Churchill Club members finally found out how they had come to be honored.

KNUD PEDERSEN: Ebbe Munck said he had sat next to Churchill on the flight crossing the North Sea from London to Copenhagen just a couple of days before. That gave him the chance to tell Churchill how and why the club was formed, about the work we did, and why we named ourselves after him. Munck told us that Churchill was moved, and felt strongly that our contribution had to be acknowledged. The moment was now—who knew when he would be back in Denmark? Round up as many of them as possible, Mr. Churchill had told Ebbe Munck. And that's how we came to be gathered—hastily—here at this hotel in Copenhagen. Although Churchill could not focus on the Churchill Club in his acceptance speech, he wished to greet us in an honor parade just before his remarks, acknowledging us much as a general passes by troops on a tour of inspection.

When the big moment came, I confess that I was absent. I missed the parade. I got separated from the group, and by mistake I went in the wrong door to the hall—in the VIP entrance where Churchill and his wife and

Winston Churchill
reviewing the
Churchill Club

the officials entered. I was only two meters from Churchill when we walked in. Our eyes met for a moment. It felt like I was looking into the devilish eyes of a confidant, eyes that almost winkingly said, "Don't believe all you hear about me."

An attendant at his side bowed slightly to me and said, "Your card, sir." I withdrew my invitation from my pocket and showed him. I hadn't read it and didn't know what it said. But whatever it was, it was magic. He returned the card and led me to a special VIP box. To my left was Prince Knud, representing the royal family. To my right was Admiral Erhard J. C. Quistgaard, chief of all Danish military forces on land and sea and in the air.

When the lights went down for Churchill's acceptance speech I slipped the card from my pocket and drew it close to see what it said that could have possibly landed me in such a high-rent district.

It was a simple business card. Below my name was my title. It was the same title that had landed me in two Danish prisons. It had inspired robotic guards to try to reduce me to a number. My title had been cursed and lauded in thousands of living rooms and kitchens and workplaces during Denmark's bleakest hours. It was a title I had taken on as a boy and would wear with pride for the rest of my life. The card read:

Knud Pedersen
Member of the Churchill Club

EPILOGUE
The Times That Followed

Churchill Club reunion, 1950, identified by Knud: "Standing, from left: Helge Milo, Jens Pedersen, Eigil Astrup-Frederiksen, Knud Pedersen, Mogens Fjellerup. Seated, from left: Henning Jensen (from Denmark's Freedom League, whose members were arrested later than us but spent their prison time in the same section as the Churchill Club). Next to him is the only one whose name I have forgotten. He, too, was a member of the Freedom League. Continuing left, Mogens Thomsen, Vagn Jensen (brother to Henning and also member of the Freedom League), Uffe Darket. The photo is taken in the garden of the monastery in 1950."

In the years after the liberation of Denmark, the experiences of imprisonment, war, and sabotage work left many of those in the Churchill Club and the RAF Club scarred for life in various ways. Here is what happened to some of them.

THE CHURCHILL CLUB'S CATHEDRAL SCHOOL STUDENTS AND YOUNGER MEMBERS

Knud Pedersen worked briefly after the war as a newspaper reporter, attended law school, and worked for a film company before devoting his life to art. In 1957, Knud founded the world's first art lending library in Copenhagen's St. Nikolaus Church, making art available to all people, rich or poor, by lending out original artworks for periods of three weeks. The fee for a loan was, at the beginning, the price of a pack of cigarettes, Knud said proudly during an interview in 2012. The Art Library still exists as an important resource in Copenhagen.

Knud's own artwork is represented in New York's Museum of Modern Art and in the Tate Modern in London, among many other collections; his work with the Fluxus art movement is collected in Denmark's State Museum of Art. Knud and his wife, Bodil Riskaer, founded the European Film College in Denmark, which has become an international success in the film world.

A Personal Note by Phillip Hoose

Knud was in his late eighties when we worked on this book. He was in fine health to begin with, but there was always a sense that we had better move fast, for we did not know how much time we had. We wrote e-mail messages back and forth nearly every day, even on weekends, me forwarding drafts from my office in Maine, Knud responding from his Art Library in Copenhagen.

Just before Christmas 2013, a week went by with no word from Knud. This was unprecedented, and ominous. I wrote again and again with no response. Finally, on January 3, 2014, he tapped out a message from a hospital bed. Pneumonia had nearly taken his life. He said he had actually felt the presence of death in his room. "I had the feeling that a shadow was walking softly around me," he wrote, "looking for a good place to get through for a final hit . . . I told it to wait, because you and I were not yet done with our work. I think our work kept me alive. Now I am fit to fight on!"

So we fought on, finishing the book in late autumn of 2014. Knud was delighted. "The first thing I did after I read it," he said, "was to forward it to my children and grandchildren." And then in early December 2014, Knud again fell silent for more than a week. On December 12, he reported from his bed, "I am losing weight dramatically and have no appetite and no energy."

After a series of tests, puzzled doctors prepared Knud for a full-body scan. The prospect of entering a narrow tube terrified him. Imprisonment at Nyborg had left him claustrophobic—afraid of being confined. Throughout his life he had refused to take an airplane or even ride in an elevator. "The doctors say that I am fragile," Knud observed in one of the last notes I received from him. "But how fragile can one be who in eighty-nine years has lived in this most cruel century anybody could dream of? I will keep you updated."

Knud Pedersen, Churchill Club leader, Danish resistance hero, and one of the most important young people in all of World War II passed away shortly after midnight December 18, 2014. He was treated as a national hero, buried in Copenhagen's Assistens Cemetery alongside other Danish figures, such as Hans Christian Andersen and Søren Kierkegaard. Knud is survived by his wife and their three children, Klaus, Kristine, and Rasmus.

Jens Pedersen was a brilliant student who gave up his resistance work to study engineering following his release from Nyborg State Prison. After graduation Jens was hired as a construction engineer by a British firm and sent to India to oversee the building of several bridges. But he became unhappy in India and returned to Denmark, where he lectured at the college he had attended. His health began to decline and he struggled with depression. Lung cancer claimed him in 1988. "He died in a hospital after a very unhappy life," said his brother Knud. "His death was the result of high intelligence combined with a low tolerance for jails and/or maybe wars." Jens had two sons, Gorm and Lars, and a daughter, Karen.

Eigil Astrup-Frederiksen (who changed his last name to Foxberg after the war) was in a German-run hospital in Aalborg recovering from his broken leg on Liberation Day. Once freed, he returned to his studies but had trouble concentrating. Like some of the other Churchill Clubbers, he had what he called "prison scars." Violent nightmares afflicted him, dreams filled with Gestapo agents. He became depressed, absentminded, and restless. His short-term memory suffered. After two years of treatment with a counselor who had other resisters as patients, he regained his health. He became a civil engineer and was able to work steadily, although his symptoms flared up again and again throughout his life. Eigil died in 2012.

Børge Ollendorff was arrested with the other Churchill Club members in May 1942, but he was too young to be jailed. Authorities deported Børge to a youth institution in a small town far from Aalborg. His attention was quickly drawn to a heavily traveled bridge between Jylland and Funen. Børge made quick plans to blow it up. But authorities caught wind of his plan when they observed his daily visits to the bridge. He was still too young for jail, so authorities moved him again. He became the leader of a small religious movement after the war and fathered twelve children.

Mogens Fjellerup, the Professor, studied economics at university and worked for the Council of Arhus, Denmark's second-largest city. He married and became the father of a son and a daughter. His daughter, Eva Fjellerup, became a world-class fencer, who participated in the 1996 Summer Olympics. Mogens Fjellerup died in 1991.

Helge Milo became an engineer first employed in Norway and later at the Lindø shipyard in Denmark. In 1971, he started his own engineering firm, working mostly with the shipping industry. He has a son, who is fifty-eight at this writing, and a daughter, twenty-three.

Uffe Darket, whose boyhood passion was building model airplanes, worked as a pilot and eventually became a flight captain on transcontinental Scandinavian Airline flights. He retired at age sixty and died in 2013.

Mogens Thomsen became a manager of one of Denmark's biggest banks. He specialized in arbitrage, the practice of buying something (such as foreign money or gold) in one place and selling it almost immediately in another place where it is worth more.

THE CHURCHILL CLUB'S
BRØNDERSLEV THREE (OLDER MEMBERS)

Alf Houlberg, *Kaj Houlberg*, and *Knud Hornbo* were the only members of the Churchill Club still in prison at the time of liberation. After having been court-martialed by Germany for removing the dummy cell bar and committing sabotage in Aalborg, they were imprisoned in Germany.

After much political wrangling between Germany and Denmark, the Houlbergs were returned to Horsens State Prison in Denmark and placed in a special unit for political prisoners. In all there were fifteen political prisoners isolated in the prison wing.

Just before Christmas 1944, a prison pastor offered to help Alf and the others escape. He gave Alf a secret plan. It would be risky, but it was a path to freedom. Alf gathered his fellow prisoners and explained the opportunity. Alf made it clear he was all for it. Every day they stood the risk of being moved to a German prison, and Alf had seen enough of German prisons. But Communist prisoners, comprising half the group, distrusted the plan. The fourteen inmates voted and split evenly—seven to seven.

The group rehashed it from every angle but remained deadlocked. Finally, a fifteenth prisoner, who had been away from his cell during the discussion, returned. Alf put it before him—the deciding vote. He was an old man, he told them; that wasn't how he wanted to die. He voted no.

Alf dutifully reported the result to the pastor but was deeply frustrated, as were the other yes voters. They told the pastor they were willing to act on their own. Alf revealed that he had been preparing to escape for some time. He had already carved a wooden pistol, which, coated with black paint, looked perfectly real. The day before New Year's Eve, 1944, the prison pastor delivered an authentic pistol to Alf and revealed the plan. At 2:44 p.m., he said, you all will be in the yard on your afternoon walk. When you hear the sound of a ladder being placed against the yard wall, run toward it. That will be your only signal. It'll be up to you to find the ladder, which will be lowered from the other side. Climb over the wall and colleagues will be waiting to drive you away. God speed.

They were all let out for their walk at 2:30. Outside the wall, a truck rolled up at 2:44. Two men clanged a ladder over the wall. Alf pulled his pistol on two of the three guards, and backed toward the ladder. A choke hold from another prisoner—a former boxer—took care of a third guard just before he could reach the alarm.

The seven prisoners went up over the wall and then down to freedom on the other side. The whole escape took only three and a half minutes.

The escapees were sent by resistance leaders to different places in Jutland. Alf was given a resistance contact in Randers and reported there. He functioned as a courier between the escapees and their contact point. Most of them wanted to go to Sweden. Alf elected to stay in the country. Why work for Denmark's freedom, he reasoned, only to go to Sweden? He became second in command for the resistance in Randers and took part in sinking two German ships.

After the war Alf became a manufacturer of plastic laminated sheets for ID cards. A series of heart attacks paralyzed him. When daily activities became too difficult and he feared he could not survive another seizure, he drove his wheelchair to the Museum of Danish Resistance in Copenhagen and donated his carved pistol to the Churchill Club collection. Then he went home and took his life.

Kaj Houlberg, the oldest Churchill Clubber, died as a young man. Knud Hornbo emigrated to the United States and became an American citizen.

THE RAF CLUB

Knud Hedelund (Little Knud, from Odense) was arrested for sabotage and spent six months in the Odense jail. After the war he enlisted in the British Army and spent several years in India. He died there at an early age.

Harald Holm joined the British Army after the war and was stationed in West Germany. His behavior became erratic. To ensure that peace would be permanent, he began to destroy stockpiles of British ammunition. The behavior earned him a bed in a mental hospital, and he was sharing a room with a Nazi collaborator when Knud Pedersen found out and got them separated.

Hans Jøergen Andersen died in his German prison cell. He was confined in an overcrowded, disease-ridden camp where prisoners were simply worked to death. Hans Jøergen's death certificate identified him as an artist and said he died of tuberculosis.

Orla Mortensen likewise died a German prisoner. Little is known about his exact cause of death. It occurred while he and other prisoners were cleaning up at a railway plant in a small German city after an Allied bomb attack.

Once captured, most other RAF Club members were sent by the authorities to Western Prison in Copenhagen and placed in a special section reserved for political prisoners and resistance fighters. Probably they were deported to Frøslev, a camp near the German-Danish border, a stop to final transport to Germany.

PEDERSEN FAMILY AND FRIENDS

Edvard and Margrethe Pedersen, Knud and Jens's parents, moved from Aalborg to Copenhagen when the Reverend Pedersen retired from the ministry. He died at age seventy-four. Margrethe lived to age ninety-four.

Gertrud Pedersen, Knud and Jens's sister, moved to South Africa, where she worked at the Danish consulate. After her husband died she moved to Bath, England, to be close to her friend Patricia Bibby. Gertrud died at seventy.

Photo of the Pedersen family in 1950, taken in the monastery's garden. Standing, from left: Jens, Knud, Gertrud, Jørgen. Front row from left: Their youngest brother, Holger, beside their mother and father

Patricia Bibby remains to this day a friend to the Pedersens and later married John Moore Heath, an Englishman who became British ambassador to Chile. She lives in England and Mexico with her children. "Pat and I are still lifelong friends," said Knud shortly before his death.

Grethe Rørbæk, Knud's prison fantasy love, went to college and received an education as a technical designer.

Aalborg Cathedral School (Danish: *Aalborg Katedralskole*) is still educating students. It is the oldest college prep school in North Jutland. Historical documents date its founding as far back as 1540. In those days, the school was housed in the wing of the monastery that became the headquarters of the Churchill Club. Aalborg Cathedral School has been rebuilt and expanded several times, most notably when it first admitted girls in 1903. There are about eighty teachers and seven hundred students at the school today.

SELECTED BIBLIOGRAPHY

I consulted many Web sites, articles, and books in writing this book. Some material was in Danish, which I translated through software applications and with the assistance of professional translators. These resources were among the most helpful.

BOOKS

Ackerman, Peter, and Jack Duvall. *A Force More Powerful: A Century of Non-Violent Conflict* (New York: Palgrave Macmillan, 2000). Shows how popular movements used nonviolent action to overthrow dictators, obstruct military invaders, and secure human rights in country after country, over the past century.

Bartoletti, Susan Campbell. *Hitler Youth: Growing Up in Hitler's Shadow* (New York: Scholastic, 2005). Explains the roles that millions of boys and girls unwittingly played in the horrors of Nazi Germany.

Lampe, David. *Hitler's Savage Canary: A History of the Danish Resistance in World War II* (New York: Skyhorse Publishing, 2011). A detailed story of the Danish resistance movement.

Laursen, Peter. *Churchill-Klubben som Eigil Foxberg oplevede den* (*The Churchill Club as Eigil Foxberg Experienced It*) (self-published, 1987). Eigil's memoir of the Churchill Club.

Levine, Ellen. *Darkness Over Denmark: The Danish Resistance and the Rescue of the Jews* (New York: Holiday House, 1986). A detailed account, structured around heroic characters, of Danish resistance to German occupation, and of the dramatic, just-in-time rescue of thousands of Danish Jews.

Lowry, Lois. *Number the Stars* (Boston: Houghton Mifflin, 1989). Classic work of fiction in which a ten-year-old Danish girl shelters her Jewish friend from the Nazis.

Pedersen, Knud. *Bogen om Churchill-klubben: Danmarks Første Modstandsgruppe* (*The Book of the Churchill Club: Denmark's First Resistance Group*) (Copenhagen, Denmark: Lindhardt og Ringhof, 2013). Knud Pedersen's account was first published in 1945 by Poul Branner and is now available in this revised and updated edition.

Tveskov, Peter H. *Conquered, Not Defeated: Growing Up in Denmark During the German Occupation of World War II* (Central Point, Oregon: Hellgate Press, 2003). Peter Tveskov was five years old when Germany invaded Denmark in April 1940. He blends vivid childhood memories with historical fact to tell the story of Danish resistance.

Werner, Emmy. *A Conspiracy of Decency: The Rescue of the Danish Jews During World War II* (New York: Basic Books, 2009). Living eyewitnesses detail acts of goodwill by people of several nationalities, including German Georg F. Duckwitz, who warned the Jews of their impending deportation, and the Danes who hid them and ferried them to Sweden.

ARTICLES

Jacobsen, Eigil Thune. "Who-What-When 1942?" (Copenhagen, Denmark: Politken Publishers, 1941).

Palmstrom, Finn, and Rolf Torgersen. "Preliminary Report on Germany's Crimes Against Norway," prepared by the Royal Norwegian Government for use at the International Military Tribunal, Oslo 1945. Available with a search on "Crimes against Norway" at Cornell University Law Library's Donovan Nuremberg Trials Collection, ebooks.library.cornell.edu/cgi/t/text/text-idx?page=simple;c=nur.

WEB SITES

www.aalkat-gym.dk is the link to Aalborg Cathedral School's Web site. The site can be translated to English, and includes source materials on the Churchill Club. See especially section 9, www.aalkat-gym.dk/om-skolen/skolens-historie/churchill-klubben-og-besaettelsen/churchill-9/.

www.kilroywashere.org/009-Pages/Eric/Eric.html will take readers to "A few personal notes on the life in Occupied Denmark 1940–45" by journalist Erik Day Poulsen. Poulsen grew up in Aalborg and went to Cathedral School a generation after the War. He has written a fine personal history, with a tribute to the Churchill Club.

natmus.dk/en/the-museum-of-danish-resistance is the link to the Museum of Danish Resistance 1940–1945, located in Copenhagen. The museum building was demolished following a fire in 2013, but its archives were saved and are still open at a new location. The museum is scheduled to be reopened in 2018.

TELEVISION PRODUCTION

Matador is a 24-part Danish TV series directed by Erik Balling, originally produced and broadcast between 1978 and 1982. It is set in the fictional Danish town of Korsbæk between 1929 and 1947, focusing on rival families. This television series so completely hooked Danish viewers that the entire series has been re-released a half-dozen times since it was first aired. It offers a fine way to understand turbulent Denmark from around the start of the Great Depression and through Nazi Germany's occupation of Denmark in World War II. Caution: The series can be ordered online with English subtitles, but as of this writing it will not play on a standard North American DVD player. You need a multiregion PAL/NTSC DVD player to view it.

RECORDINGS

The BBC broadcast of Danish liberation can be heard on YouTube at www.youtube.com/watch?v=78pDhZb8hZo.

www.youtube.com/watch?v=zKSj_zOfOw8 provides over an hour of German marching songs such as those Knud Pedersen heard in the streets of Odense and Aalborg.

The opening page of the Churchill Club's story in the September 1943 issue of *True Comics* (see also page 136)

NOTES

The first-person accounts in Knud Pedersen's voice derive from personal interviews and e-mail messages. Knud and I recorded interviews in Knud's office in the Copenhagen Art Library each day between October 7 and 14, 2012. We spoke for nearly twenty-five hours in all, generating hundreds of pages of typed transcript.

When I returned home to the United States, we communicated by e-mail. Though Knud and I lived nearly four thousand miles apart, if I sent a question to him in the midafternoon Eastern Daylight Time—9:00 p.m. in Copenhagen—he would usually have a reply waiting for me when I arrived at my laptop the next morning. The deeper into the book I got, the more precise my questions became, and the more revealing Knud's answers. When something didn't make sense to me, I enjoyed the luxury of simply being able to ask a living protagonist to clarify seventy-year-old events. For example:

> Phil: When you torched the wagon full of airplane parts, you say
> you used a magnesium "plate." I don't understand what this
> "plate" is or how it works. Can you help me clarify this?
> Knud: The disc itself was made of magnesium. It was flammable by
> the use of a match. It did not explode. It burned but with an
> extremely clear flame.

During the course of two years, we exchanged nearly one thousand e-mail messages.

A third source of information is Knud's published writing. Before his death, Knud was one of only two surviving Churchill Club members—the other being his Cathedral School classmate Helge Milo. Knud was the Churchill Club's principal spokesperson from the very beginning. In May 1945, just after Denmark's liberation from the German occupation, a publisher contacted Knud's father seeking the opportunity to publish a book detailing the true story of the renowned Churchill Club.

Edvard Pedersen relayed the offer to Knud, who put it before the other club members (except for his brother Jens, who was away at university). He asked, "Is this something we want to do? If so, how shall we go about it?" There was general agreement that it was worth doing. Each Clubber solemnly agreed to write a chapter and read it aloud to the group when they met again in two weeks. But when they reconvened, only Knud had written anything. Knud read his piece aloud, to applause. "Why don't you just keep going?" said his mates, and so he did.

Edvard Pedersen arranged to have a secretary type the finished manuscript, but—unbeknownst to Knud and his club mates—he had the typist cross out all the curse words just before publication. This angered the group when they finally saw the book, published in Danish in 1945 with the title *Bogen om Churchillklubben* (*The Book of the Churchill Club*). It was revised by Knud and reissued by several different publishers over the years.

Knud supported his narrative by publishing police records and military documents. He became a dogged and creative researcher. He found photos and newspaper accounts, digging up an incontrovertible record of the group's pioneering impact. He unearthed ministerial letters, correspondence between German and Danish authorities, prison documents, and newspaper accounts. He amassed an unusually rich trove of images—cartoons, photos, headlines. He made this material freely available to me and helped me sift through it since the treasure is entirely in Danish.

All this is to say that by far the richest source for this book was Knud Pedersen himself. A week of interviewing in Copenhagen, the hundreds of e-mail messages we exchanged, and translations of the books he wrote in Danish so long ago—these were the prime sources that this very lucky writer had to draw from.

In addition, Clubber Eigil Astrup-Frederiksen (who later changed his name to Foxberg) wrote his own account of his Churchill Club experience in a 1987 book in Danish, whose title translates to *The Churchill Club as Eigil Foxberg Experienced It*. It is especially helpful in describing the boys' incarceration at Nyborg State Prison. Churchill Clubbers Helge Milo and Mogens Fjellerup have also been briefly quoted in published sources.

Patricia Bibby Heath, who developed a special friendship with Knud after his release from prison, granted me a telephone interview of a little more than an hour on April 26, 2014.

The notes here present sources of information used to supplement the material derived from Knud Pedersen. Abbreviated source references refer to works cited in the Selected Bibliography.

1 OPROP!

12 Operation *Weserübung*: For insight into the German invasion of Denmark and Norway on April 9, 1940, see www.nuav.net/weserubung2.html. Also see C. Peter Chen, "Invasion of Denmark and Norway, 9 Apr 1940–10 June 1940," ww2db.com/battle_spec.php?battle_id=93. Chen's article includes an extensive timeline of Operation *Weserübung* and a collection of over fifty photographs.

15 The Invasion of Norway: An extensive description of Germany's invasion of Norway and Norway's response can be found at Wikipedia's page "Norwegian Campaign," en.wikipedia.org/wiki/Norwegian_Campaign.

2 THE RAF CLUB

17 stories of Norwegian civilians being murdered by German troops: See Palmstrom and Torgersen, "Preliminary Report of Germany's Crimes Against Norway."

19 Hitler Youth: See Bartoletti, *Hitler Youth,* for an excellent treatment of the Hitler Youth movement.

20 RAF: See the documentary film "The Battle of Britain," narrated by Ewan and Colin McGregor (Toronto: BFS Entertainment, 2011), available on DVD.

22 Hitler and Bicycles: Niels-Birger Danielsen. *Werner Best* (Copenhagen: Politikens Forlag, 2013), pp. 274–75.

3 THE CHURCHILL CLUB

26 Why the Aalborg Airport Was So Important: During the course of the war the airport was expanded enormously. More than two hundred farmers were relocated, and the farms adjoining the airport were taken over by the Germans. Hangars, repair depots, and command posts were erected in haste and camouflaged to look like barns and farm buildings. At the peak of Germany's Norwegian campaign, 150 planes of several types, the majority being Stuka dive bombers, attacked locations in Norway from the Aalborg airport. They also served to protect submarines stationed along the piers in Aalborg and German ships traveling between Norway and northern Germany. For more about the airport and the sabotage efforts of another young resistance fighter in Aalborg named Frode Suhr, see Lyle E. Davis, "The Making of a Spy," *The Paper*, December 17, 2009, www.thecommunitypaper.com/archive/2009/12_17/index.php.

27 Holy Ghost Monastery: See en.wikipedia.org/wiki/Hospital_of_the_Holy_ Ghost,_Aalborg.

29 Cathedral School: The school where six of the Churchill Club members studied has a fine Web site that includes material on the Churchill Club, www .aalkat-gym.dk.

4 LEARNING TO BREATHE

39 Danish folk songs . . . "King's Badges": See Ackerman and Duvall, *A Force More Powerful.*

41 The Limfjorden Bridge: Aalborg and the neighboring town of Noerresundby are separated by a fjord—a long, narrow, water-filled inlet with steep sides or cliffs, created by glacial erosion—known as Limfjorden. During the war, the two towns were connected by a road bridge and an iron railway bridge. Because the strategically important Aalborg airport is on the Noerresundby side, armed German soldiers guarded access carefully with checkpoints on both ends of the bridges. Visit the Limfjord Museum's Web site for more information about the waterway: www.limfjordsmuseet.dk.

5 FLAMES OF RESISTANCE

50 Marie Antoinette had used the same code pattern: Hans Jøergen Andersen and Jens Pedersen developed a code for sending sensitive messages between the Churchill Club in Aalborg and the RAF Club in Odense. It was based on a famous code used by Marie Antoinette and her friend Count Axel von Fersen of Sweden in their secret correspondence during the French Revolution. For more, and an example of how the code actually worked, see www.h4.dion.ne.jp/~room4

me/america/code/fersen.htm. For background about Count von Fersen and Marie Antoinette, see en.chateauversailles.fr/history/court-people/louis-xvi-time.

7 WHIPPED CREAM AND STEEL

61 eastern front: In August 1942, Hitler's huge Sixth Army fought Russian troops at the Russian city of Stalingrad. That was the key battle of the eastern front and a turning point of World War II. Over five months of brutal fighting, Russian forces held on to Stalingrad and then turned the tables on their Nazi enemy. There are many Web sites about this brutal battle. A fine book is Antony Beevor, *Stalingrad: The Fateful Siege, 1942–1943* (New York: Viking, 1998).

64 Kristine: Lovely photos and lush remembrances of this, the classiest bakery in Aalborg and the favorite of sweet-toothed Nazi officers, to be found at www.face book.com/media/set/?set=a.205034729522481.61915.203935242965763&type=1.

12 KING HANS GADES JAIL

96 Rector Kjeld Galster: Kjeld Galster, *Aalborg Cathedral School During the Occupation* (Aalborg, Denmark: 1945).

96 Some students rose from their seats: See the source materials on the Churchill Club at the Cathedral School Web site, especially section 9 (www.aalkat-gym .dk/om-skolen/skolens-historie/churchill-klubben-og-besaettelsen/churchill-9/).

103 Kaj Munk: For more information about the life and activities of Denmark's best-known playwright and most famous supporter of the Churchill Club, see www.kirjasto.sci.fi/kajmunk.htm.

13 WALLS AND WINDOWS

108 The Nazis had . . . allowed Sweden to be officially neutral: Here is a link to a good discussion regarding why Germany did not invade Sweden and instead allowed the nation to be officially neutral: en.wikipedia.org/wiki/Sweden_during_World_War_II.

113 songs about Hitler: There were hundreds of anti-Nazi songs during World War II, many obscene. Some derided the "big four" Nazi leaders—Hitler, Goebbels, Himmler, and Göring. For a broader treatment of the songs of World War II, see www.fordham.edu/halsall/mod/ww2-music-uk.asp.

15 NYBORG STATE PRISON

125 "I missed my mates": See Laursen, *Churchill-Klubben som Eigil Foxberg oplevede den*, p. 46.

129 "His tone was apologetic": Ibid., pp. 56–57.

129 The Telegram Crisis: See Ackerman and Duvall, *A Force More Powerful*, p. 218.

133 August 29, 1943: Ibid., p. 221.

134 The turning point for Denmark: See Ackerman and Duvall, *A Force More Powerful*, p. 230; Levine, *Darkness Over Denmark*; and Tveskov, *Conquered, Not Defeated*.

135 The Rescue of Danish Jews: The quickly organized boatlift of most of Denmark's Jews to safety in Sweden is Denmark's proudest moment during the war. Many accounts have been written. In particular, see Ackerman and Duvall, *A Force More Powerful*, p. 222; Levine, *Darkness Over Denmark*; and Lowry, *Number the Stars*.

16 FIRST HOURS OF FREEDOM

139 The factory was an obvious target: There are two versions of who was responsible for the factory arson in Naesby. One is as Knud and Jens Pedersen learned it from Knud Hedelund at the party in Odense, and has been reported in these pages. A second account comes from records of communist saboteurs working in Odense. As the resistance movement became better organized and spread throughout Denmark, activists tried to recruit members of the RAF Club because—though young—they were experienced saboteurs. Communist partisan groups—known as "p-groups"—were especially persistent. But the RAF was unwilling to be controlled by anyone, especially planners from the Soviet Union. The RAF turned the Communists down, causing bad blood.

The two groups met quite by accident at the factory on the night of the fire. By pure coincidence, both the RAF Club and the communist p-group had planned to torch the same factory at the same time. Hans Jøergen Andersen later reported that he set the fire, accompanied by three other RAF Clubbers. Two p-group members told a newspaper reporter in 1995 that, no, it was their group that had set the factory ablaze.

"I have given my version," noted Knud Pedersen. "I think it is just fair to note that there is another version."

17 BETTER ON THE INSIDE

146 Patricia Bibby had wanted to meet Knud Pedersen: Author's April 26, 2014, interview with Patricia Bibby.

148 The SOE: See Knud J. V. Jespersen's English-language account *No Small Achievement: Special Operations Executive and the Danish Resistance 1940–1945* (Copenhagen: University Press of Southern Denmark, 2002).

151 "My name is Helge Milo": Cathedral School Web site, www.aalkat-gym .dk/fileadmin/filer/import/Churchill/Kilder/kilde_16_og_17.pdf.

152 Eigil found himself accepting: See Laursen, *Churchill-Klubben som Eigil Foxberg oplevede den.*

153 His spirits plunged: Author's April 26, 2014, interview with Patricia Bibby.

155 Gertrud Pedersen, Patricia Bibby, and Inger Vad Hansen: Resistance Fund-raisers: Ibid.

157 Liberation!: For more about the Danish Liberation, see Levine, *Darkness Over Denmark*, pp. 139–45, and Tveskov, *Conquered, Not Defeated*, pp. 85–91.

ACKNOWLEDGMENTS

I thank Peggy Akers for helping me locate translators of Danish text to English. Her greatest find was her mother, Gertrude Tuxen, who at the age of ninety-six wrote out translations of dozens of pages. Thanks, too, for the fine translation work of Linda Tuxen.

Thanks to Carol Shanesy for typing dictated passages and to Kathren Greenlaw for transcribing more than twenty-five hours of recorded interviews between Knud Pedersen and me.

I extend my gratitude to Phebe Tice and Samuel Kemmerer, students at Breakwater School in Portland, Maine, for carefully reading the book in manuscript form and commenting extensively. Thanks to their teacher Cheryl Hart for finding them for me. I thank Dean Harrison for superb tech support, keeping me and my laptop going through several generations of change. Thanks to Mark Mattos of Curious City for emergency Web support when I was most baffled.

I thank my wife, Sandi Ste. George, for sharing every aspect of this project. She let me read aloud to her chapter after chapter, commenting along the way, and then listened to the entire book several times. She shared my excitement as this book came to life. I am a lucky man.

At Farrar Straus Giroux Books for Young Readers, Macmillan Children's Publishing Group, I thank Roberta Pressel for yet another fine design and Simon Boughton for his faith in and support of this project. Special appreciation goes to my editor, Wesley Adams. Creative, insightful, and responsive, Wes had an intuitive sense for the content of this book and a talent for solving problems.

I thank Patricia Bibby Heath for kindly and thoughtfully sharing with me in a rather hastily arranged telephone interview the dramatic events and personal experiences of seventy years ago.

In Denmark, the staff of the Museum of Danish Resistance steered me to Knud Pedersen and thus can stake a claim on the origin of this book. Niels Gyrsting kindly provided many of the images that enliven these pages and document the story. Karen Nielsen helped me find Aalborg resources. Knud's daughter Kristine Riskaer Povlsen helped keep the project going, especially when her father was ill. His son Rasmus Riskaer Smith also contributed timely technical assistance. Knud's wife, Bodil Riskaer, provided unwavering support of this book in countless ways. Val and B. Bach Kristiansen kindly assisted with research and translation.

When one contacts the Art Library in Copenhagen, one reaches Mette Stegelmann. Mette shared with Knud and me the day-to-day work of this project. She was the go-to person when we needed help with photographs, contract work, or rushing a message across the Atlantic. She is a joy to work with.

Knud Pedersen was one of the most remarkable and inspiring people I've ever met. The chance to work daily with Knud to tell this important but too-obscure story of World War II was a lifetime thrill. We concluded each of the hundreds of e-mail messages we exchanged with the word "love." At least on my part, I surely came to mean it.

ILLUSTRATION CREDITS

Aalborg Katedralskole (Aalborg Cathedral School): 31, 96

Bjørn Erikson: 65

CORBIS: 129

Estate of Knud Pedersen: 21, 30, 70, 100, 106, 113, 127, 147, 149, 167, 174

Nationalmuseet/Frihedsmuseet (National Museum of Denmark/Museum
of Danish Resistance): 8, 10, 11 (photograph by H. Lund Hansen), 14,
26 (photograph by Scherl Bilderdienst), 40 (photograph by John Lee),
44, 46, 57, 60, 63, 79, 104, 122, 134, 135, 142 (photographs by G. C.
Krogh), 148 (photograph by G. C. Krogh), 157, 158, 160, 161 (photograph by Jørgen Nielsen)

Niels Gyrsting Collection: ii, 13, 18, 27, 35, 38, 43, 47, 49, 51, 52, 67, 76, 82,
88, 94, 103, 111, 116, 118, 128, 130, 136, 140, 162, 165, 180

Sandi Ste. George: 2

Wikipedia: 72

INDEX

195